A
Sidelined
Coach

RIDING OUT THE CORONAVIRUS

John C White

Charleston, SC
www.PalmettoPublishing.com

A Sidelined Coach

Paperback ISBN: 978-1-63837-219-6
eBook ISBN: 978-1-63837-220-2

Prologue

*F*or many years, players on my various high school teams have told me that they would like a compilation of my stories in written form. Coupled with the fact that my grandsons live 2,000 miles away from Oregon in western Texas, it became apparent that it would be an excellent vehicle to pass along history. I think it is always important to know where you came from, so I have included some of my family history as well as my own.

My stories have been the result of a long playing and coaching career that has taken place over 65 years. I have played many different sports and coached for many years, including a stint running a baseball school for a professional minor league team. As a result, there are many stories.

I normally use these stories to pass along the lessons that sports provides. I speak to my athletes about staying in the moment, perseverance, hard work, training the mind, and loving what you are doing. I tell them that in the end it becomes the journey, not the destination, that you most remember. I tell them stories to help build relationships.

I want them and my grandsons to know that out of the low spots in life come the greatest successes. I want everyone to know that the youngest, smallest, most bullied can rise to great heights. I also want them to know that some of their most long lasting relationships can come from sports or the other things that they truly love. That's what I have attempted to do with this book. If I can reach even one of those I am attempting to reach, it will be a success. It is my hope that those who read this book enjoy it and take something from it that makes their lives better.

This short book is dedicated to Lloyd Campbell who died from a brain tumor shortly before I completed writing. Shortly after he died, it was announced that the Blitz Weinhard Men's Fastpitch team and myself individually were to be inducted into the Northwest Region 9 (Oregon, Washington, Idaho, Montana, and Alaska) USA Softball Hall of Fame. The team was also announced as an inductee into the State of Oregon USA Softball Hall of Fame. Lloyd would have been thrilled with those awards that we share together.

Chapter 1

As the spring of 2020 unfolded without baseball, softball, track and field, and golf being played for the first time in my 68 years on earth, it suddenly became a time for reflection. There were questions that needed to be answered. Like, what values have I gained by participating in and teaching sports? How can I continue to teach values to my athletes and others? What are some of my favorite memories? Are sports really a necessary part of recovering from the Covid-19 pandemic? Do I have the passion and energy level to coach another 10 years, to make an even 50?

Being a high school coach goes far beyond coaching a club team, it is much more like being a teacher. The values taught are many, but the one that really provides the biggest advantage in life and during this pandemic is probably perseverance. Being able to bounce back when life throws you for a loop is invaluable. It is inevitable that life is going to knock each of us down occasionally, no matter what our chosen path may be. Sports teaches us to come back stronger on the other side of those setbacks.

When kids reach high school it can be a rude awakening. For the first time in their lives they have to work for playing time. There are often 4 classes of school trying to play on two teams, varsity and junior varsity, then they have to be better at a position than others to get significant playing time. For many, it is their first encounter with real life. And, to top things off, they have to attend school, get grades, and behave themselves to play, too.

Nobody knows what life can throw at you. There are good times and tough times. In the end, it becomes how you bounce back from the tough times and challenges that really counts. Life is a roller-coaster that sometimes goes in directions that could never be imagined before being confronted. It is full of stops and starts, backing up and taking a new path, brick walls and beautiful journeys.

For some, facing those setbacks is very difficult. They look around for someone to blame, often not taking the time to reassess themselves. This is a mistake. Until a person can take ownership of who they are right now, it is hard to improve.

I am a dyed-in-the-wool Eagle Point Eagle! I grew up in Eagle Point, Oregon, went to school there for 12 years, knew the fight song by 4th grade, and after college and 4 years in the Air Force, I came back and coached 7 years of either baseball or softball. After that, I went away to other places to coach, but I am now in my 7th year of another coaching stint at EP, all softball. To me, Eagle Point is an awesome place, but we do have problems. One problem is that we tend to lose good athletes to other schools.

Often, the problem has nothing to do with what is going on at Eagle Point. I like to call it the "Grass is Greener"syndrome. It happens in most places in this country but it's very pronounced in our area. There are about 15 high schools in the Rogue River Valley of southern Oregon. Eagle Point is not the biggest school, but it is far from being the smallest. And, that is where the problems begin. The biggest problem with all this is that the central part of the valley has the biggest schools and the jobs. Parents from the bigger schools continually talk to the parents from Eagle Point, socialize with parents from Eagle Point, and recruit for the bigger high schools. They often say such things as "our school offers better opportunities and curriculum". It happens more often with the best athletes and has for more than 60 years to my knowledge.

There are issues for the kids with this scenario. In most instances (but not all), the athlete who gets recruited does not become the great savior they hoped to be. They don't become leaders like they had hoped. The opportunities are seldom greater in the new place. In fact, they tend to leave a void at Eagle Point. It gets filled, but many times not at the same skill level. When they arrive at the bigger school, they have to find new friends, don't spend as much time with the friends they grew up with, and get swallowed up by the system. They go from being a big fish with leadership opportunities to being just one of the fish. When I talk to college coaches, they often ask about leadership when recruiting a player. They are far more interested in the player who sticks it out to lead their team to better places than they are in the nomad who is always trying to find that better place for themselves. Those who choose to search will tend to jump from college to college later on. Stability is what most college coaches want. They will find athletes like that no matter where they go to high school. Parents, athletes, classmates, and even people in the community hear the same recruiting scenario from other high schools to the point that it becomes an ingrained truth even though it seldom is true at all.

I have watched this scenario play out countless times. In fact, it was part of my youth. St. Mary's High School, the local Catholic High School, recruited me when I was in 8th grade. They had arranged transportation, sent several athletes to talk to me, offered me a scholarship, and told me how much better St. Mary's was than Eagle Point. I also had Crater athletes pushing me toward attending Crater. I held out and I'm really glad I did. I became team captain in baseball and basketball, leading me to feel a larger responsibility for success of my teams, and making me raise the level of my own game.

My very good friend, Ray Peterson, did not hold out. My junior year, Ray was our sophomore quarterback and starting catcher. Our football team was a state semi-finalist, losing only to state champion

Central High School. Ray was good, very good. Of course, he ended up at Medford High School the following year. He and his dad moved to a house that was suddenly contributed, his dad was offered a job, and the two of them moved into Medford. His mom and sister, Mikie, stayed at their home in Shady Cove. Mikie, a senior that year, was angry about her dad not being around. It put a real strain on the family. Even though Ray split quarterback duties on a state champion team, he confided to me later that he wished he had stayed at Eagle Point.

High school sports is more than X's and O's. It becomes the place where athletes begin to dig deep inside the mental part of the games played and deep inside their own mental make-up. I am most passionate about baseball and softball because those sports have so many episodes where an athlete is tested both mentally and physically. Mental strengths and weaknesses are revealed as are physical strengths and weaknesses. Sometimes, because of the compression of the classes, that revelation of weaknesses is hard to overcome. But, more importantly, it is possible to build themselves better after failure. It is a very important time in a person's life because it allows an athlete to build success from failure. Perseverance is the key.

Many factors influence high school athletes. Some play because they have friends who play. Some choose to play because their parents want them or force them to play. Some play because they have always been better at the game than teammates. Some play because that's what they have always done. But, the ones you want are the players who play because they love the game. Those players will typically, but not always, continue to get better, will have infectious enthusiasm, have a tendency to have a great practice attendance rate, have a higher ceiling as a player (many will go on to play in college) and will typically be good teammates.

Even if players are playing because they love the game, there are many factors that can hold them back from being successful. Some of those factors are parents who support too much or not enough. Players need to learn to make their own way, but they need support from their parents, too. The very best players make decisions quickly and can't afford to look around for direction.

Having a job during a season is another issue, even if the job is babysitting. Time management and communication becomes critical.

Another key element is the tendency to procrastinate or make excuses. I have had some players who have made excuse after excuse to miss practices. Others put schoolwork off until beyond the last minute and then rush to get it done. Time management can help relieve the pressure that gets created.

Friends can be problematic, too. Friends who are a bad influence are visible to everybody, but even well-intentioned friends can create difficulty. They can add demands to a player's time. There is nothing more important than the time spent with the team. Players seem to believe that practicing on their own is okay. In reality, it sets them apart if these practices are in place of team practices because learning to be a team is one of the most important aspects of what is taught by high school sports. Just showing up is more important than anything.

High school athletes have many demands. They get pulled in many directions. And, with the Covid-19 pandemic, every single day has had a big question mark beside it. The athletes who have been getting better every day will arrive on the other side in fine shape. Those who have let things slide, will not.

Chapter 2

S ome of the challenges I have faced will be shared later, but first I would like to share some of my favorite experiences, a life that has revolved around sports. My memories are many, but here are a few of the best.

The first involves a trip across northern Texas. I was driving back to Goodfellow Air Force Base in San Angelo from a Sunday semi-pro baseball doubleheader. Suddenly, it began to rain really hard. That usually wasn't a problem because the roads in Texas are crowned to allow run-off. I was in the middle of a 90-mile stretch with no towns and very little traffic. It seems that all the larger towns in Texas are 90 miles apart. As I was driving along, the road began undulating in the distance...just like the movie Tremors. The road was moving! And, it didn't stop as I got closer. It was starting to freak me out a little. I was at a loss to explain it and thought about turning around until I finally realized that I was driving through thousands of tarantulas jumping up and down to keep from drowning. I hurried through that stretch of road...crunch, crunch, crunch. They had congregated on the road because it was the highest point. Evidently, tarantulas congregate once every couple years in a big colony. I found it.

Most of my best memories in fast pitch softball were team related, but there are a few personal memories that stand out. In 1978, I was picked up by a team sponsored by Roseburg Merchants to play in the ASA (now USA Softball)Northwest "A"Regional tournament in Spokane, Washington. In those days, men's fast pitch was very popular. The girl's game was also popular, but only 8-10 travel teams existed in the Northwest. It was before Title IX had a good start and softball did not exist in most high schools or colleges.

The regional tournament went well for the Roseburg team and I was on fire hitting. I had 10 hits through our first three games. We won the first two and lost game three in a close one. After the third game, the team manager approached me and asked if I was okay with sitting out the next game. I told him that it wasn't a problem because I was a pick-up player and was just there to help his team. Besides, B-1 Bombers from Fairchild Air Force Base were flying over every few minutes. It was fascinating watching those monstrous planes fly over with their wings flapping up and down.

The pitcher for the other team was tough and so was Tom Huff, our guy. The game went into the 11th inning tied. The manager came up to me in the bottom of the 11th and told me he was going to have me pinch hit. I grabbed a bat and started to the on-deck circle. When the guy I hit for found out he had been lifted, he went ballistic even though he was 0 for 5 with three strikeouts. He started screaming at the manager and quit the team right there. He threw his gear into his bag, grabbed his wife and children, and began walking around the outfield fence to the parking lot in center field. Right about then, I stepped into the batter's box and crushed a long home run that landed about 10 feet in front of the departing family. Walk off! Mike Cornutt picked me up at the plate and carried me all the way to the dugout. We went on to win the regional and I was the tournament MVP. The guy who quit did not get to experience that win or the 8 days all-expenses paid trip to a lakeside condo on Lake Tahoe for the National Championship Tournament. We finished 7th out of 54 teams and had a blast. Mike and hard-hitting George Decker later played for our Blitz team from Medford for many years and we experienced great times together.

In the early 1980s, I was asked to go with a local Medford team to a big, annual tournament in Redding, California. The pitcher off my regular team, Mike Trotter, was asked, too. Some of the best pitchers in the world were regular attendees of that tournament and that year was no exception. When we arrived in town, I picked up a Redding Searchlight newspaper. When I opened up the sports section, there was something I have never seen, before or since. There was an entire page (with no ads) devoted to the pitcher we were facing that night, Chuck D'Arcy. The article talked about how he had just finished winning the National Sports Festival in Colorado Springs and the Pan-American games pitching for the USA. It also stressed how dominant he had been, how he had amassed an astronomical number of strikeouts, and that he was on a 63 inning scoreless streak. He was widely recognized as the best pitcher in the world at the time.

Trotter and I were stunned at the number of fans who turned out that night. It was later estimated that 5,000+ people were there, a huge turnout for softball and a bigger crowd than we played in front of during the 1981 National Championship quarterfinals against the local Redding team.

As Chuck warmed up, the fans started buzzing at how fast he could throw. There were plenty of oohs and aahs as he went through our line-up the first three innings. He struck out everybody in the order on three pitches, except me. His rise ball was devastating, but I managed to hit a weak pop-up to second base for the third out of the first inning.

By the time the 4th inning came around, he no longer respected us. He had developed a pattern of rise ball at the knees, rise ball at the waist, rise ball at the armpits, sit down. I was the 12th batter he had faced. He had 10 strikeouts and I was the only one to have touched the ball. I was watching closely and went to the plate with a few thoughts in mind. First, I was going to look for that very fast rise ball at the knees. Secondly, I was going to make sure that my hitting mechanics were perfect. Then, I was going to relax because relaxed is quicker.

Sure enough, everything worked out perfectly. I got that low rise, my swing was perfect, and I sent what the gun had as the equivalent of a baseball being thrown 105 mph, out of the park in dead centerfield. As I dropped the bat and started running to first, I realized that D'Arcy was looking at me with an icy stare, all the way around the bases! When I got to third base, the third baseman had his back to the pitcher. He had a big grin on his face and mouthed the word "Nice" as I passed him. I continued to the plate and the dugout without looking at Chuck. When I got to my teammates, Trotter had a huge smile and said "That was awesome"! And, it was. But, it got better.

When I came up again in the 7th inning, D'Arcy had been altering his pitches for two innings. Again, I had been watching closely and had determined that the hard drop was probably his second best pitch. Knowing that he probably wasn't going to throw me the low rise, I looked for the drop. I dropped the bat head on the ball and just crushed a hard ground ball single between short and third.

When I got to first, I looked up to see Chuck D'Arcy, the best pitcher in the world, walking off the field. When he got to the foul line, he threw his glove over the dugout, then went and sat down in the corner, without a second pitcher being warmed up. The crowd was stunned and so was I. Somehow, one of my most memorable personal moments had been in a 9-1 loss!

Chuck D'Arcy finished his stellar softball career by coaching pitchers for Arizona State, University of California-Berkeley, and the USA Women's team.

Another softball memory required me to just be in an observing role of a remarkable event. The New Zealand National Team was on a tour of the west coast. New Zealand produces some of the best teams in the world and always has great pitching. Our very strong 8-team league in Medford was to provide two teams to play a Wednesday night doubleheader. It was decided that whoever was in the top two positions in the league would play. Only, there was a problem. Our Blitz team and D&D Radiator were tied for second behind the Malot Mudhens.

The league decided that 6 players from Blitz and 6 players from D&D would combine to play the Black Shirts in the second game, facing legendary pitcher Kevin Herlihy. When the team was picked, I was on it, but our second baseman was not. Evidently, he had told a lot of people that he was going to play. When he walked away after finding out he was not playing, he was muttering to himself and was clearly upset.

When game day arrived, there had been all kinds of promotion and fanfare. There was a big article in the newspaper the day before and several thousand people showed up, including our second baseman...in a hard ankle cast and on crutches! He was telling people that he would have been playing except he had torn ligaments in his ankle. We all felt bad for him. After all, torn ligaments take 6-8 weeks to recover. He wasn't going to get to play much for the rest of the year!

Despite playing well and collecting 6 hits, we lost 6-3. Later that evening, as we visited with the New Zealanders, they told us that we had hit Kevin better than anyone on the tour. We also got our Blitz guys together to decide who we might pick up to play in our weekend tournament in Yreka, California. On Friday of that week, we made the hour long trip to Yreka and started to warm-up. Guess who shows up in full uniform, ready to play? That's right, our second baseman had made a miraculous recovery! We all shook our heads at what had happened, but he played lights out until the championship game. The championship game started out well and going into the 6th inning, we were up 3-2. We got two outs, but there were runners on first and second when the other team's best hitter hit a ground ball to second base. It was right at our second baseman. He didn't have to move, a very simple play. It went right through his legs and rolled slowly to the fence. Both runners scored. When I looked up, our second baseman was hopping off the field on one foot. True story, I swear!

Lloyd Campbell and I were very good friends. We and our wives would spend a lot of time together.

Lloyd was one of our pitchers in the Jackson County Softball Association and at one time had a 100+ game win streak in league even though he was never considered a flame-thrower. He was pitching for the team I was playing on, Lithia-Allen, on the day he turned 30 years old. So, we decided we were going to send him a gorilla-gram. A guy locally had a gorilla suit and would show up at special occasions, take a microphone, snap off a witty poem about his target from information he gathered from us, bestow a few gifts, and then would depart to a round of applause. Before the game started, we took the field and were warming up when the gorilla arrived. He walked right out on the field and started in on Lloyd. A pretty good crowd was there that night and everybody had a good laugh at Lloyd's expense. I think it shook Lloyd up a bit because he grooved the first pitch to the lead-off batter who promptly belted it out of the park. Lloyd did manage to compose himself after that and didn't give up another hit the rest of the game.

Chapter 3

As I mentioned earlier, my best memories involved team successes, mostly involving our legendary hard-hitting Blitz team. In 1980, we had the experience of a lifetime and then followed it up the next year. A lot of things had to come together to make that first success possible. The first happened a week before the Oregon ASA state tournament. Jimmy Moore, who played for D&D Radiator, dumped his motorcycle and got a little banged up. Our team was very good, but we didn't have a dominant pitcher like Jimmy. We beat him a couple times that year, but he was getting better every time we played. I remember one game during that season against Jimmy. He was beginning to be the dominant pitcher he would later become. He had the best drop ball I ever saw and had developed a spectacular change-up that was impossible to pick up. I came into that game in the middle of the only slump I can ever remember having. During my first swing, I discovered my timing was really messed up. So, I decided I would bunt. And, I did. Knowing that I had a reputation for hitting the ball hard, the infielders were deep. I dropped a bunt down...to the shortstop, and beat it out. Jimmy just looked at me and told me I could never do that again. So, the next time I came up, I did it again. I never told him that I was trying to bunt down the third base line both times... and much softer. And, I didn't tell him that he was the only pitcher I ever gave in to because I wasn't able to hit him that day. As tough as Jimmy was, we were going to have a tough time being one of the three teams that advanced to the Regional tournament in Billings, Montana from the Oregon State ASA tournament in Eugene.

At state, we lost one of our early games and battled back through the loser's bracket. By Sunday morning, we had won our way into the game that would determine the final regional spot. Our opponent would be D&D. We had been watching Jimmy all weekend. He was hurting, and we could tell he was wearing down. I realized from my first at-bat that he didn't have his best stuff, but he was highly competitive and worked his way into the lead by the 4th inning. Then, the 7th inning happened! Jimmy ran out of gas, and we exploded. We scored 6 runs to take the lead. We knocked Jimmy out of the game and kept hitting against his replacement, Neal Ellis. I had a great game, collecting five hits. In the end, we won the game 7-6 and won our way into the regional.

As we were sitting in the shade making plans to get to Billings, one of our pitchers took offense to something that was said and tried to kick Larry Binney in the head. We immediately took a vote and kicked the pitcher off the team. That solved a problem, but left us short a pitcher. We had already decided to ask Jimmy to go with us and had asked him as we walked through the line after the game. He agreed. But, it meant that he would have to shoulder more of the load. We had two weeks to get him recovered. By that time, he was raring to go and so were we. We cruised through the regional in 5 straight games (all wins by Jimmy) and earned a trip to the ASA National Championship in Oswego, New York.

One problem, it's a long way from Medford, Oregon to upstate New York and it was going to be expensive. Our sponsors told us they would pick up a lot of the cost. And, there was a bunch of interest locally for what we had accomplished. The local radio personalities, including the future voice of the Oregon Ducks Jerry Allen, put together an exhibition game against us that drew several thousand people. We were able to cover all expenses for the trip.

When we got to Oswego, we discovered that it was a hotbed of fast pitch softball. They had men's, women's and youth fast pitch... a total of 160 teams. The fields were on the parade grounds of Fort Oswego, which was a Revolutionary War fort on the west facing bank of Lake Ontario. It was a very cool place and is a national monument.

The first thing that left a lasting impression was the opening ceremonies, where 54 teams from throughout the country were introduced one by one. We were introduced next to a very cocky team from South Bay, California. They walked in talking about how they were going to cruise through the tournament because they were such a great hitting team. We didn't say much but we were paying attention.

On the second day, we played the opener very poorly and lost a very close game. On day three, we met the South Bay team. They had lost on day one, 1-0. So, we proceeded to shut them out again, 3-0. Jimmy was brilliant. Having lost two straight and not scoring a run, South Bay went home with their tail between their legs.

We started getting hot after that, and kept winning every day. The fans started adopting us too. They loved that we were beating teams from traditionally strong states. They loved that we dived for everything. They made up chants to support us, and chants to put down our opponents. When we went out to eat, the local restaurants didn't charge us. We signed autographs. By the time we got to the championship day, probably 80% or more of the crowd was behind us.

We had to beat a very strong team from Orrville, Ohio to reach the finals. Late in the game, with the score tied at 2, I hit a two-run home run to put us up by two. I was 16-22 at that point, the best hitting National tournament for average in my career. Jimmy shut them down from there to put us in the championship game. The fans were going nuts.

For the championship game, the fans just poured in until there was no seating left. Our opponent was S H Goode from Pennsylvania. It was a major battle. All of a sudden, balls that were falling in before found leather. I kept hitting at 'em balls even though I was still hitting the ball hard. Finally, in the 6th, I hit a double, my first hit of the game and tied the game at 2. It stayed that way until the 10th. We had chances. Jim Chubb got thrown out at the plate. Everybody was making plays. We were putting pressure on every inning, but could not score. In the 10th, the Pennsylvania team got their lead off guy on, on a walk. The next guy bunted and reached first on a bobbled ball at first. Both guys moved up on a passed ball, so we intentionally walked the next batter. Then, Jimmy struck out the next two guys...two outs and the bases loaded.

That meant that their best hitter was going to be coming to the plate. He hit a ground ball between George Decker and I...George missed it by an inch and in a picture ever etched in my mind, I did too. We were both stretched out parallel to the ground. It was heartbreaking and we all walked off with tears in our eyes. Jimmy was MVP of the tournament. I went 1-4 in the final game to end up 17-26, .653, losing the batting crown to a guy who went 9-13, .692. Gary Glass and I joined Jimmy on the All-American team. Mike Cornutt and George Decker were second team. And, maybe the best part, the residents of Oswego, New York threw us a party all over town... for finishing second! They loved us and we loved them.

Jimmy ended up getting a job offer and a spot on Peterbilt Western's team out of Seattle. They became the best team in the United States (also sponsored by Pay n Pak in later years). Jimmy went on to become the best pitcher in the world over a 5 year period. I was offered a spot on that team as well, but chose to stay in the Medford area because I had a wife and two-year old daughter.

In some ways, the next year was a much better year. Jimmy was gone to Seattle but Mike Trotter was with us from the beginning.

Coupled with Lloyd Campbell and Duke Anderson, we had a formidable pitching staff. We blasted through the league and won tournament after tournament. And, we won the Jackson County Softball Association Championship for the first time. Four more followed in later years, but the first was very memorable. Mike Cornutt and George Decker arrived from Roseburg about 10 minutes before game time in the game to determine the championship against Malot Mudhens. We were almost on the edge of panic because they weren't there. So, what happened? Mike laced up his shoes, threw a few tosses back and forth, then promptly went out and hit 3 solo home runs to lead us to the league title 4-0. When the regionals arrived, we were on a 22 game winning streak. So, we were pretty confident. But, the regional championship in Boise, Idaho was far from easy. We got the best other teams could offer and had to struggle to get to the finals. For three straight games, we went into the 6th inning down by two runs. And, in all three games we got a three run home run to pull out the game, from three different guys. From then on, we always talked about the "Blitz 6th". That was our inning.

In the finals, we faced a team from Spokane that was 81-3 on the season. They had an incredibly quick team, good pitching, and they executed well. But, we gained the psychological advantage in the first inning. Their lead off hitter Avon Meachem got on base right off the bat. He had already stolen every base he had tried in the tournament and had over 100 steals on the season without being thrown out. Sure enough, he took off on the first pitch. Warren Cooper, our high energy catcher, threw a seed to me at the second base bag. I was standing at the bag holding the ball before he even started to slide. I tagged him standing up. He was stunned, his team was stunned, and they didn't try to steal again.

Lloyd was on the mound for us. He had been used somewhat sparingly in the 1980 Nationals because Jimmy was so hot. This time around had not been so easy. Our pitching staff was stressed.

Every game had been a battle. The plan was for Lloyd to start and then relieve him when we needed to get him some help. What nobody knew is that this game was extremely important to Lloyd. He had confided to me on our trip to Boise that just once he would like to be on the mound when our team won a regional or national tournament. This was his chance. He gave up a first inning run and then nothing more. The final 10 outs were pop-ups and when the final out settled in a glove, Lloyd leaped into the air in a shot captured in perpetuity by the Boise Statesman newspaper. We had forged an 8-1 win, and captured a spot in the Nationals again, this time in Redding, California.

We felt pretty good going into the tournament and played very well the first couple games. In fact, there was a buzz going around that we were the team to beat. On Friday night, we played Holiday Erlanger, a Redding team that had been loaded up just to be host team for the tournament. We had played them multiple times during the year. We were slightly ahead of them in wins and losses for the year, but they were very good.

The crowd was huge and loud for our game and it was tight all the way. In fact, Holiday was tied with us at 1 going into the 6th inning. We had the top of the order up and knew it could be our last chance. We came out firing. Ron Webster led off with a single. He moved up on a groundout by BJ Rodgers. Then, I singled to put us up. Mike Cornutt singled. Then, Gary Glass homered to deep left into a large group of his former high school teammates to put us ahead 5-1. And, that's the way it ended. We were flying high, with only one more win needed to reach championship Sunday.

The problem was we were a very emotional team and had trouble coming down from our high intensity win of the night before. Coupled with the fact that it was 2 am when we finished and had a noon game the next day, many of us were sluggish for our game against Lake Lillian, Minnesota. And, we played like it. By the time we woke up, we had lost 2-1 to a team that was far inferior to the team we had beaten the night before. We lost again that night to Guanella Brothers and finished 5th in a tournament that we should have won. Gary and I were on the All-American team again. In a turnaround from the previous year, Gary hit .643 and I was around .500. Warren Cooper was second team.

Chapter 4

*N*ot all softball memories occurred on the field. One story that will never be forgotten by anyone who was there was the famous(or infamous) team bonding fishing trip on the Rogue River above the small village of Union Creek. The place we decided to camp involved a hike of about 2 miles on a well traveled and improved trail. The hike was fairly flat, but there were about 15 bridges in between the road and the campsite.

As we gathered our Lithia Allen players and their gear, the wife of our coach Jim Hughes pulled me aside to tell me something unusual. She told me that no amount of sound would wake Jim if he fell asleep. She also said that he wouldn't wake if you shook him. The only way he could be woken was a nose tickle. I was thinking no way, but it proved to be totally accurate.

Four of us got our fishing and camping gear together and headed for our rendezvous at the trailhead. It was 1975. I had just gotten accepted to Southern Oregon University, was a newlywed to my first wife Rachel and Wild Rainiers were running through the forests in a popular beer ad. This was before cell phones, but we had our plans all laid out ahead of time.

We arrived a little earlier to the rendezvous than the agreed upon time. The second group arrived shortly after. One of the guys in the second group said it was going to be a little bit of time before our last guy, Ronnie, was going to show up because he went to pick up a surprise.

It kept getting later, and later, and later. Ronnie still was not there. But, finally just before the sun went down, here he came around the bend pulling a horse trailer. He got out of his truck with a huge grin on his face and proudly announced "I brought us some help". One of the guys asked whether he had brought a mule. He told him that it wasn't a mule. It was a jackass!

We were thinking that it was a pretty good idea and quickly loaded the animal with our heaviest items. When he was all packed up, we started down the path...until we heard a shout from behind. Ronnie and the jackass were still standing where we left them. And, the entire pack had shifted and was hanging under the animal's belly. So, we went back, reloaded, and redistributed the load. As we were moving cans of food from one side of the pack to the other, the jackass got a name. From that point on he was known as Ronnie's Ass!

We headed out again, with Ronnie and Ronnie's Ass taking up the rear. We reached the first bridge and went across. Once again, we heard a shout from behind. Ronnie's Ass would not cross the bridge no matter how hard Ronnie pulled. By this point, it was dark. We all had flashlights, but it was still pretty dark. After another delay, Ronnie guided Ronnie's Ass down through the muddy wash and up the other side. This happened another 14 times with the entire group breaking out in guffaws each time we crossed another bridge. Ronnie and Ronnie's Ass were covered in mud.

Finally, after a couple hours, we reached the flats. Suddenly, our guide (the only teammate who had been to this spot) pulled up and said that he thought we had gone a little too far and he would need to go check. He left his pack with us and started toward the river, which we could hear off to our right 100 yards or so. Suddenly, his flashlight disappeared and we heard the famous Butch Cassidy line "Oh, S**t" as he also disappeared from our sight. Several of us went over to the spot and found him at the bottom of an 8 foot bank in a pit, covered in mud. By now, we were all laughing so hard it was hurting to breathe.

Eventually, we made it to the campsite, set up our tents, blew up our air mattresses and laid out our sleeping bags. Then, we opened up canned chili, fried some potatoes, added cheese to both, and opened a couple beers each. It was a good meal, but it was guaranteed to create lots of gas. We then went to bed, with the idea that we were going to get up early to go fishing. I was in a tent with my high school friend Jim Chubb, and my best friend Lloyd Campbell. Lloyd was legendary for the smell of his gas. About 4am, I woke up gagging. The air was putrid and looked green inside the tent. I put my nose near the floor of the tent, dragged my bedding out the door and slept outside the rest of the night. If not, I may have died.

We got up early the next morning, cooked and ate breakfast. Then, four of us went upstream to a small logjam that had been a fishing hot spot the previous year. We were hopping from log to log and started catching some nice 10" native trout. ..until Jim Chubb stepped on the wrong log. The log he stepped on was not jammed in with the rest and it started rolling. He fell off and went into the icy river. We were at about 5000' elevation, and even though it was midsummer, it was not warm. He went in up to his chest before we grabbed him and pulled him out. He decided it would be prudent to go back to camp and change clothes. But, Alex Bergin, Lloyd, Mike Johnson, and I stayed and kept fishing until each of us found our own rolling logs and decided that maybe it was too dangerous to be out on that particular logjam.

The three of us started the hike back to camp when something caught my eye. At a random spot on the river in a shallow sandbank, we found the den of the Wild Rainiers! Sitting on the bottom of the crystal clear pool were two cases of Rainier beer. There were no Rainier parents anywhere and there were no humans, either. So, we hauled it back to the camp. Imagine the surprise when we walked into camp with fish and Wild Rainiers.

After a nice lunch of fried trout and hash browns, we were just sitting around the fire talking and laughing about all the crazy things that happened on the trip when I looked over at Jim Hughes. He had folded his sleeping bag in half. His legs were in the dirt. His upper half was on the bag and he was sound asleep! So, I told the guys what his wife had said about how soundly he slept and how difficult it was to wake him. Nobody believed it, but several guys decided they wanted to check it out.

Lloyd and Ronnie had brought their pistols along with them. A plan quickly evolved. They would stand close to Jim and fire their guns at the beer and chili cans from the previous night that they would set up on a log. When Ronnie fired his .38, Jim did not stir. So, Ronnie fired again. Nothing. Ronnie shook Jim, still nothing. The guys set the cans up on the log again. Up stepped Lloyd. He didn't have a quiet little gun like a .38. He kept telling Ronnie that he had a man sized gun, a .45 caliber and it was loud. Sure enough, when Lloyd pulled the trigger, it was a boom that reverberated through the forest. He shot again and again...boom, boom, boom. The cans were destroyed, but Jim didn't move. In fact, he started snoring! So, the ideas started flowing again.

One of the guys found a short forked stick. He pushed it into the ground between Jim's legs. Then, he took a couple bullet riddled cans and put them on the forks of the stick. After that, he had Lloyd and Ronnie stand right beside Jim with their guns pointed down by their sides. Then came the big tickle. A short fir bough did the job. Jim sort of pawed at his nose, then woke up. As he began to turn over, he noticed the cans and then the guns. He turned as white as a ghost. We couldn't contain ourselves any longer and burst into laughter. The guns had never been unsafe, but Jim probably still thinks they were shooting at the cans that were 8" above his legs. The rest of the daylight hours were uneventful. We went fishing again, came back, had a good meal, laughed for hours and finally went to bed.

But, we didn't sleep. As we were starting to drift off, I got a nudge in the side from Lloyd. He asked me if I could hear a noise. I listened closely and there it was, the oddest sound I had ever heard... somewhere between a moan and a scream "Woooaaaaa"! It was far off but it seemed to be getting closer with each utterance. We had no idea what it was...a ghost? A rabid animal? A wolf? No clue! For an hour, we kept hearing"Woooaaaaa", getting closer and closer. We could not identify what it was, but we did know that we were miles from anywhere and other than a couple pistols, we were close to helpless. Finally, after an anxious hour, the noise was right outside our camp! And then, just as we became the most worried, the noise started receding until it was no longer heard in the distance. When we got up in the morning we went searching for clues. We found some scat and tracks right outside our camp. The tracks appeared to be those of a medium size brown bear. The noise? It appeared that the bear had a bellyache because it had been eating green huckleberries (wild blueberries).

And, still, the camping trip would offer even more events beyond that crazy Saturday. When we got up on Sunday, a bunch of the guys took off to go fishing. Lloyd and I stayed at the camp, just hanging out. We were just sitting there talking, when Lloyd gets this little grin on his face. He told me he was going to shoot at a wasp nest that was hanging down under a fallen log on the far side of the river. I tried to talk him out of doing it, but he had his mind made up. He raised the gun and fired. It looked like he missed, but a couple wasps came out and were circling around the hive. Lloyd raised the gun and fired again. This time quite a few more wasps came out of the nest. They didn't circle, they headed straight for Lloyd!He started running, but they were catching him. Finally, he dropped his gun in the dirt and kept going. The wasps stopped at the gun and circled. Luckily, Lloyd got off scot free, thankful that he hadn't been caught.

Our trip back from this legendary fishing trip was not quite as eventful, although Ronnie's Ass still refused to cross bridges. No one who was there will ever forget that particular weekend.

Chapter 5

In 1969, my senior year, Eagle Point High School experienced a breakthrough year in baseball. For years, we had come up short against Henley High, but not that year. We went into the series with Henley that year with a lot of optimism. We had tough pitchers, Bill Thurman and Dan Reed. We were in the third year of Fred Herrmann's coaching tenure and we were solid defensively.

The deciding game was tight throughout. Henley pitcher, Roger LaFlash, and Bill Thurman matched each other pitch for pitch. I tripled and scored in the first inning. When I came up in the 5th, we were down 2-1 and there was a runner on first, fellow senior Jim Chubb (my backcourt sidekick on the basketball team). I hit another triple to deep right center at the VA Domiciliary field. Then, another senior, Randy Dover ripped a single to centerfield to put us up 3-2. Bill bore down after that to get the win. All four of the seniors, Bill, Randy, Jim, and myself had pulled more than our weight to get that breakthrough win. We had all been playing together for many years and that win has been a source of pride for us all until this day. In succeeding years, the Eagles have been part of the conversation in baseball in the local area for more than 50 years.

College baseball at Southern Oregon University was a highlight period of my life...except the first four weeks of my sophomore year. I was incredibly excited about being able to play college baseball again, but had a major mishap on my first day of baseball practice. I had been putting in a lot of time in the batting cages and the weight room. I had also been playing city league basketball all winter, which turned out to be a mistake in judgement. Our league championship basketball game was on the first day of baseball practice. I decided to go after a mind debate with myself. I ended up tearing ligaments in my left ankle. The doctor put me in a hard cast and told me he would see me in 6 weeks. I was not a very good patient. I tore the cast off after 4 weeks, had the college trainer mummy tape my ankle every day and started being a designated hitter. I was able to begin playing defensively in a couple weeks, but I wasn't 100% until summer. Yes, I loved playing baseball.

Danny Miles was a hero of mine growing up. A Medford native, he played football, basketball, and baseball at Medford High School and at Southern Oregon College (later SOU). He was an incredible athlete. He was 4 or 5 years older than me, so when I went back to college at SOSC (first SOC, then SOSC, then SOU...same school, different names), Danny was coaching at Oregon Institute of Technology, OIT. Even though he would become a legendary basketball coach in later years, Danny was also coaching baseball when I got to Southern Oregon. And, my first college baseball memory involved him.

Late my sophomore year at SOU, we were playing our bitter rival, OIT. We were down by a run when I came up in the bottom of the 9th with a runner on second and one out. I hit a double to right center that scored the tying run and went to third on the throw to the plate. The next guy hit a medium depth fly ball to left that I tagged on and took off for the plate. Billy Fagan, the catcher, was a tough guy and had the plate blocked. As he started to raise up to catch the ball, I slid into him...hard! He caught the ball as I hit him and it sent him into a cartwheel over me. Danny exploded as the umpire called me safe, with the ump saying that I reached the plate before Billy tagged me on the way down. The argument went on for a long while, but we won the game! Billy later became a very good assistant softball coach at OIT. The double I hit that day was one of 18 I hit that year, a school record for a season (we played around 35 games a year).

My junior year included a feat that happens very seldom, maybe close to never, at any level of baseball or softball. It started with a first pitch solo home run to right by left-handed hitting Danny Stockel, followed by a first pitch solo home run to left by right-handed hitting Ernie Tacchini. I stepped in to the box next with a hard act to follow. But, I managed to do it. The pitcher threw a fast ball right down the middle and I blasted it out of the park in dead center field. We had gone back-to-back-to-back on three consecutive pitches to begin a game, to all three fields! Our next guy, Marv Woods, got drilled square in the back on the first pitch. I'm glad I wasn't hitting 4th!

We nearly had our baseball season stopped that year for all of us. On a trip to Western Oregon, we were split up in two 15-passenger vans. The Head Coach, Gary Nelson, drove one and the other was driven by an assistant coach. I was in Coach Nelson's van. When we got to Monmouth, there was a representative of the State Education Department waiting for us. Evidently, one of our outfielders had mooned the Director of Higher Education from the assistant coach's van. We got the riot act read to us and ran a bunch of wind sprints the next week, but we didn't lose anybody off the team.

We went on to play in the NAIA district playoffs in Portland, but came up short. We played both our games in the rain and were slipping and sliding around, not a great experience.

My senior year was an awesome time. Gary Glass spent the year spouting witticisms, mostly directed at me, but no one escaped them. We laughed constantly, enjoyed playing the game, needled each other mercilessly, and won the league. We also beat a number of Division 1 teams, including a thrilling 3-2 win over Oregon at Miles Field in Medford and a doubleheader sweep of the University of Portland. The Oregon win featured a defensive play in the 8th inning that happens very seldom. The Ducks had runners on first and third and attempted a double-steal. Steve Acevedo gunned the ball to me at second. I swipe-tagged the runner from first, spun and gunned it back to the plate for a double play.

It was a great senior year. A couple moments stand out. The first was a little frightening. We were playing OIT in Klamath Falls. I hit one of the hardest balls I ever hit...right back at the pitcher's face! Somehow he fell backwards, the ball clipped the bill of his cap, and went on one hop to the center fielder. An inch lower and I could have killed him. I can still see that in my mind.

We wrapped up the league title with a 3-game set against OIT where our hitters went ballistic. We just kept scoring. Kevin Aguirre, Gary Glass, Steve Azevedo, Harry Mauch and I were all on fire. Guys were on base in front of me every inning. I ended up driving in a bunch of runs and it resulted in the most productive series of my college career.

One thing that is always brought up by ex-teammates when we talk about our baseball years is how crazy it was east of the mountains. It was sort of like the Wild West when we went to Eastern Oregon or Eastern Washington. Several incidents stand out. The first happened during my junior year. When we arrived in LaGrande for our Friday afternoon game against Eastern Oregon, the stands were packed and the fans were really rowdy. There were no rules in those days about noisemakers and it was not often that an administrator was present to control the actions of the crowd. Consequently, it got crazy. Every time we came up to bat, the cow bells were in full force...hundreds of them... and the name calling was atrocious. In particular, they were relentless toward our pitcher, John McLaughlin. He quickly acquired the moniker "Orca, the whale". He was a big guy, but he was very good. And, he shut them down despite the noise. Some of our guys were affected, but it didn't seem to bother me. I went 4-4 and hit the ball hard. The next day, we played a doubleheader and lost both games. I was still hot at the plate and when I came up for the third time in the second game, I was 10-10 in the series. Every at bat, there had been constant sound from the crowd. The 11th time was different...complete and total silence! Someone had gone through the crowd, telling them the cowbells were not working against me so they needed to try silence. I just crushed a ball to left. Their left fielder went back to the fence, jumped, and caught the ball. My last at bat was more of the same silence. Again, I crushed a line drive...right at the third baseman. The result was a huge cheer from the fans both times.

When we got back to our motel, we were not in a very good mood. But, we took showers and got dressed, then went to find something to eat. It turned out that LaGrande didn't have many places that were open after 7 pm. In a group, we walked for half a mile trying to find something. The only place that was open and served food was a country western bar/restaurant. We went in, ordered food and drinks and all sat at a long table. The place was packed with cowboys. The food was good, but Jeff McDonnell was not satisfied with the music. He asked the DJ to play some rock and roll. After several tries, he started to get frustrated. He came back to the table muttering to himself. When John McLaughlin came back from the rest room and told us he had punched a guy out who had asked him if he had seen that "Orca" who pitched for Southern Oregon the day before, we decided it was time to go. As we got up to go, Jeff picked up one end of the table. Plates, drinks and food slid off the other end onto the dance floor. We quickly exited the building and walked through the parking lot that was filled with pick-ups, all with rifles in the rifle racks. We split into small groups and made our way back to the motel even though there were several loaded pick-ups searching for us.

The following year, we took a trip to Eastern Washington. We were the Oregon Evergreen champions. Eastern Washington was the

Washington champion. The three game series was a best-of-three to determine the overall champion. We won the first game on Friday to put us one game from winning it all. Unfortunately, that was not to be. We made it through about 4 innings before the roof caved in. We gave up a bunch of runs and lost fairly badly. All the while, there was a large crowd of college kids gathering on a hillside in left field. They had trucks backed up towards the field with kegs flowing. It became a very long day as we were getting crushed in the second game. We were out of pitchers and were pitching position players. All of the action began to center on the hillside. Beginning in the 4th inning, we were getting mooned by guys every time we took the field. By the 6th inning, girls were getting involved too. Some of us found it amusing, but some of our guys were getting angry. In the bottom of the 7th inning, things got out of control. Our center fielder decided he was going to get involved. As he arrived in center, he dropped his pants, then one pair of shorts, then his sliding shorts, then his jock, then another pair of shorts. Finally, he began to moon the crowd in left. They gave him an ovation, but Gary Nelson, our coach, was on a dead run toward him. He yanked him from the game (after he got dressed).

As the inning progressed, we were getting drilled. Our catcher called timeout. He told the coach that he was getting tired of the trash talk that every batter was feeding him as they came to the plate, and he wanted to pitch. The coach gave in and our catcher, Steve Azevedo, took the mound. He hit the first guy, then the second guy, then the third guy! Eastern's coach was livid. He jumped out of the dugout, rushed to the third base line and began to yell at Vedo. Vedo just looked at him, then pointed at him and said "You, get a bat and then pop off!". The umpire went out and talked with Steve. He did stop hitting guys, but he did shut them down too. We managed to get out of town without incident, but we were a little anxious on the way out.

I ended my too short college time with a home run in my final at bat at the NAIA District playoffs. Unfortunately, we lost the game and were eliminated from a chance to advance to the NAIA Regionals. But, we had a great year that year. And, all-in-all my time at SOU was a very satisfying time in my life.

As I sat there alone, reflecting on the finality of my final game at SOU, two of the most respected NAIA coaches in the Northwest approached me. My former coach at Pacific, Chuck Bafaro, and the longtime coach at Eastern Oregon, Howard Fetz, were there to apologize to me. They had just come from the regional coaches meeting. They both expressed their disappointment that I was not going to be nominated for All-America status because I was a little older than the other players and they were angry. They told me that every one of the coaches agreed that I was the best player in the region, but they had been outvoted about who to nominate. The younger coaches wanted to make a push for those players they felt had a chance to sign professional contracts. Needless to say, I was disappointed, but it felt good that they had made a point to find me and let me know what happened.

Chapter 6

I don't remember it personally, but my passion for baseball was kindled on my first birthday. That was the day my grandpa, John Lucas, gave me my first ball and glove. After that, not much else mattered. I sat in front of the television with my grandpa on Saturdays and watched cartoons followed by the weekly baseball game. It seemed like it was always the Yankees or the Giants. So, my early heroes were Mickey Mantle and Willie Mays, still two of the greatest who ever played. In my early years, I bounced balls off concrete walls and caught them, hit rocks, ran the bases and played countless hours of imaginary baseball, all because I talked baseball with my grandpa.

John Lucas, my namesake, was an impressive man. Born in 1883 in the Ozark Mountains of Arkansas, he left home after the 8th grade to follow the crop harvest with his 16 year-old brother, Walton Hood Lucas (they called him Hood). The two of them, 13 and 16 years old, worked their way all the way to the apple orchards of Michigan before returning to Arkansas for the winter. At home, they hunted wild hogs, squirrels, and wild turkeys for food and raccoons for fun. They went fishing. They did this for 3 years, traveling all the way from Arkansas to Michigan each year. Mostly, the two of them were able to fend for themselves. They had to because the family was huge. There was a total of 12 kids.

John and Hood's mother was half Cherokee. Her family had owned slaves in Georgia before making their way west during the civil war. She died in childbirth after her 6th child was born. Their step-mother also had 6 kids. According to my mother, Patricia Lucas White, the step-mother was the most superstitious woman who ever lived. Mom and her brother Bud terrorized her in later years. They would tie thread to the rocking chair and pull on it from another room. They would concoct ways to throw shadows around a room without anyone being there. They would put up ladders in awkward places. They were very creative and consistently freaked her out.

John Lucas was a master storyteller and he lived a fascinating life. Consequently, my mother became a storyteller as well. She may have been the smartest person I ever met in my lifetime. She went back to college while I was in high school, obtained her bachelor's and master's degrees, became a high school English teacher, then wrote 14 published novels in a variety of genres...fantasy, historical romance, western, suspense, etc.

Some of John Lucas's best stories were about baseball. He often told the story of whittling his own baseball bat one winter (whittling and storytelling were hand-in-glove with grandpa). He religiously whittled and sanded his bat until it was perfect for him. He looked forward to the first game between his town team and a neighboring town. On the appointed day, he walked 10 miles to get to the game site.

Upon arrival, it was discovered that there were only two baseballs. Each team used one to warm up and then the game began. My grandpa was a mask-less catcher, but he never got to catch or hit a ball that day. The first pitch was fouled into a massive blackberry patch and the second pitch followed into the same patch. After searching for hours without success, the game was called off. My grandpa grabbed his bat and walked the 10 miles back home...all scratched up from the blackberry vines.

He also talked about playing against the father of Hall-of-Famer Dizzy Dean and brother Paul Dean, both major leaguers in the

1930s. Town teams were the order of the day around 1900 and whole communities came out to watch. It was big entertainment because there was no radio or television. It was the gathering place for everyone in the area. And, it was the reason baseball became the national pastime. During the early 1960s, Dizzy Dean and fellow Hall-of-Famer Pee Wee Reese were the voices of the Saturday MLB Game of the Week. My grandpa and I always watched.

In addition to baseball, John lived a highly eventful work life. The first event occurred in 1899 when he was 16. He was hired in Ft. Smith, Arkansas to become a Deputy Sheriff in Oklahoma Territory. I have no proof, but I like to think that he became associated with Bass Reeves, the black Sheriff who became the model for the Lone Ranger. Bass Reeves was responsible for the capture of more than 3,000 criminals. Oklahoma Territory was a place where criminals hung out after committing robberies and other crimes in surrounding states. The law men from those states could not follow them in to Oklahoma, but the Federal Sheriffs could. They would arrest them and take them back to Ft. Smith where Roy Parker, "The Hanging Judge", awaited them. In grandpa's first days in this atmosphere, things got really hairy. He was staked out in an Oklahoma saloon waiting for a known criminal to come in the door. He was sitting at a heavy oak table in the corner of the room when their mark came in. The guy recognized them immediately and had both guns out. Grandpa had the presence of mind to flip the table and get behind it. Luckily for him, it was just in time to stop the bullet headed for his head. They got the guy, but Grandpa quit the next day.

It wasn't the last time he got shot at or the last dangerous job he held. In the early 1900s, the oil fields scattered around Texas were made up of a number of small operators. The job sites were often very hazardous, even to the point of having multiple people die. Grandpa got a job working on an oil drilling platform somewhere in eastern Texas. His future wife, my grandma, Lee Cook, was working as a cook in the mess hall. Both of them had a friend who got killed on one of these wildcat rigs. My grandpa felt like it really could have been avoided with safer equipment. He started talking to union organizers and soon became one himself. He was chased, had to fight, and was shot at on multiple occasions. But, he was instrumental in effecting safer working environments in the oil fields.

After Grandpa and Grandma married in 1917, they got out of the oil business and headed to California, probably with Hood, to work for the Madera Sugar Pine Company. By the time the Great Depression started, Hood had died and members of both the Cook and Lucas families were living in the west. Hood, by the way, was the grandfather of George Walton Lucas Jr of Star Wars fame. My family never had much contact with George's side of the family after Hood died because everyone seemed to go in different directions.During the depression, some family members stayed in the Bakersfield area and other parts of the Central Valley. Others worked their way north, including my grandparents. My mother was born around this time in Hanford, California.

Grandpa worked as a supervisor on a Civilian Conservation Corps (CCC) crew that built bridges in Yosemite National Park before finally settling on B Street (now Shasta Avenue) in Eagle Point, Oregon in the 1940s. Members of both the Lucas and Cook families settled near Eagle Point as well. He eventually retired after running a crew that paved Highway 62 from Medford to Prospect... in sections of poured concrete mixed on site.

The Lucas family ended up in Arkansas after originally settling in northern Virginia. The original Lucas family home, built in the 1500s, still stands in Wales. The Cooks landed in Texas after stops in North Carolina and Alabama. They originally came from Ireland well before the Potato Famine. They were in Texas before it became a Republic and well before it became a state. All in all, ancestry has our family being connected to at least 15 of the people on the Mayflower. We have connections to both Jamestown and Plymouth Rock. And, we have Dutch and Huguenot heritage that helped settle New Amsterdam, in later years known as New York.

Chapter 7

When the Lucas family arrived in Eagle Point, the other side of my family had been in the Rogue River Valley for nearly 100 years and had their own set of interesting stories.

My great-great-great grandfather Aaron Chambers, his son William, and their families signed up for free land in Oregon Territory under the Homestead Act of 1850. They arrived in Table Rock City (now Jacksonville)soon after and began farming at least 320 acres on nearby Hanley Road. Table Rock City was quiet in those days, but not for long because gold was discovered in the area in early 1852. The Chambers family probably arrived by wagon on the Applegate Trail. The Applegate Trail split off the California Trail in Nevada after the California Trail split off the Oregon Trail at Ft Hall in present-day Idaho. Before the Chambers family came west, they were descendants of the Chambers clan that founded Chambersburg, Pennsylvania.

An interesting story still survives in Chambersburg, a town that was started with religious tolerance in mind at a time that such things did not exist. The problem was there was only one structure large enough for services of all the churches that settled there. Eventually, the Chambers family sold land to the Presbyterian Church. The payment was to be a single rose from the church garden each year to be given to the Chambers family patriarch. After 250+ years, the custom still exists, the only known arrangement of its type in the world. Chambers family members rode with George Washington as officers during the Whiskey Rebellion in western Pennsylvania, the first collection of taxes in the United States.

Table Rock City was renamed Jacksonville and became a pretty hopping place soon after the Chambers family arrived. Not only were miners pouring into the area, the natives were also trying to live their lives (with little success) and the town was growing fast enough to become the county seat. Some of the mining outfits also brought Chinese coolies to dig ditches and move water for mining operations. And, the US Cavalry opened a small outpost called Ft Lane about 5 miles to the north, near the Rogue River.

The cavalry tried in vain to get the miners and the small bands of different tribes to make peace with each other. But, some of the miners had other ideas. While the native males were at the fort talking about a peace plan, a group of rogue miners massacred a native camp of women, children, and the elderly near what is now Eagle Point. Needless to say, the native men were pretty riled up. They banded together and took off to the west. As they crested a mountain, they came across the Harris homestead near what is now North Valley High School. They killed the two hired hands immediately, and wounded Mr George Harris. He managed to get back to the cabin to warn his wife before he died.

Mary Ann Harris, the wife, and her young daughter Anna Sophia managed to keep the natives at bay for a whole day by firing two guns from windows at opposite sides of the home. Mary Ann's son, who had spent the night at a friend's house and was walking home, was never found. But, Mary Ann and her daughter were discovered hiding out by a cavalry patrol the next morning. They were taken into Jacksonville, where Mary Ann was given a home and hired by one of the founders of Jacksonville, John Love, to look after his elderly mother. John Love married Anna Sophia when she turned 16. They had four children, two boys and two girls. When my great-great-great grandmother, Wata Ann Chambers, died in 1859,

Mary Ann and Aaron became close and eventually married. When Anna Sophia and her youngest daughter died during a smallpox epidemic, Aaron and Mary Ann raised the other daughter, Mary Harris Love. Mary married into the Hanley family and was a fixture at Hanley Farm (also called The Willows) until her death in 1904. Her two brothers moved to Eastern Oregon where both died at an early age. Her daughter, Mary Love Hanley, became the founder of the Southern Oregon Historical Society. Aaron and Mary Ann's home is a national historical landmark and still stands at the corner of 3rd and C St in present-day Jacksonville. The Hanley Farm is also designated as historical and is a major fixture in the Jacksonville area.

My great grandfather, William Chambers Jr, married into another established local family when he wed Lucinda Obenchain. John Obenchain Jr, Lucinda's dad, owned a stage-stop on the military road from Ft Lane to Ft Klamath that had been started by his father, John Sr. The location was about halfway between the current towns of Butte Falls and Eagle Point on what is now Obenchain Rd. An interesting assortment of travelers passed by on the Military Road, including annual trips by natives from east of the mountains as they brought wagon trains of grain to be ground at the Butte Creek Mill in what is now Eagle Point. And, John's brother Madison, called Mat by most people, would drop by as he traveled back and forth to his ranch in eastern Oregon. As of this writing, seven generations of the family have eaten pancakes made from flour ground at the Butte Creek Mill. (Note: As of this day, the mill is being historically reconstructed after a major fire). John Jr was the first postmaster, innkeeper, restaurateur, and head of a school in the area near present-day Butte Falls.

John Sr had quite a legacy of his own. He was famous in the area in early years for his teams of horses that pulled logs from the forest and hauled freight back and forth across the mountains and around the valley. He died in 1884.

The home that belonged to John Jr's brother Bartlett and his wife Nancy Obenchain in Jacksonville is also on the historical registry and is just a few blocks from the Harris-Chambers home.

William Chambers Jr built a hotel in Butte Falls on speculation that a railroad was going to be built to transport passengers to Crater Lake. Because of a number of factors, including the increased use of cars and the development of Highway 62 from Medford to Crater Lake, the main rail line only made it as far as Butte Falls. He never made the big money he anticipated and the railway never became a great passenger experience. But, it was used for many years to transport passengers and logs from Butte Falls to Medford.

Lucinda and William's youngest of three daughters was Arline, my grandmother. Arline married my grandfather, Charles Omar White, and they started their family in Butte Falls. Charlie's parents had married in Illinois and had moved to the area. His dad, George, ended up getting sick. He moved back to Illinois, leaving his wife Lola in Oregon. He died in Illinois, probably from tuberculosis, and Lola remarried. I never knew Charlie. He died in a freak accident near Ashland, Oregon shortly before I was born. The car in which he was a passenger slid off the road, rolled on to its side and trapped him under water in a creek. He drowned before meeting most of his many grandchildren.

My dad was also named Charles, Charles William White. He was born in 1930, so his early years were spent during the tough years of the Great Depression followed by World War II. He grew up tough and was always a hard worker. He scraped for everything he acquired and he held on to it tight. Unlike my mother who encouraged me in every way, my dad found fault in everything I did. He was a real paradox to me. He would praise females to the heavens, but my brother and I could never do anything right. An example of this was the night my high school basketball team upset number one ranked Rogue River, a team that featured two future Oregon

State players, Gary Schontz and Ron Jones. I scored 17 points that night and pulled down 12 rebounds in a 51-49 game. I was excited and on the way home I thought maybe I had finally done something that would impress my dad. When I walked in the door, the first thing he asked was why I had missed free throws.

I can never remember my dad congratulating me about anything, ever...not when I got married (either of the two times), not when my 3 great kids were born, not when I got straight A's in high school or college, not for numerous baseball all-conference awards in high school and college, not for softball All-American awards, not for Oregon ASA Softball Hall of Fame, not for being on the same All-State team as my son Kelly in 2009 (me as a coach and Kelly as a first baseman), and certainly not for any times my teams won at anything...playing or coaching. He was no longer alive when I was inducted into the Southern Oregon University Hall of Fame for baseball, but he wouldn't have been impressed with that either. All of that being said, I wouldn't trade the experience of growing up with my parents with anyone raised on positivity alone. My mom built me up, and my dad tore me down. Each time I got stronger and the education I received from the process was invaluable.

1981 BLITZ WEINHARD AT THE "CLASS A" NATIONALS IN REDDING, CA.

CRATER LAKE SCHOOL, 1903, JOHN OBENCHAIN JR, SCHOOLMASTER

Eagle Point High School Softball 2019

Harris-Chambers Home, 3rd and C St, Jacksonville, OR

Jimmy Moore, the best Men's Fast Pitch pitcher
in the world in the mid to late 1980s

John Obenchain Sr Gravesite, Jacksonville, OR. Also interred in this historic cemetery are Aaron Chambers, Mary Ann Harris Chambers, John Obenchain Jr, and numerous other family members

JOHN WHITE AND LLOYD CAMPBELL, COACHING 2017

KELLY WHITE (1ST BASE) AND JOHN WHITE (COACH) FATHER-
SON DUO ON THE 2009 OREGONIAN ALL-STATE TEAM

Obenchain Stage Stop 1883

Paige Leeper, Grandslam in NAIA, National Championship Game

143

SOU Baseball 1978

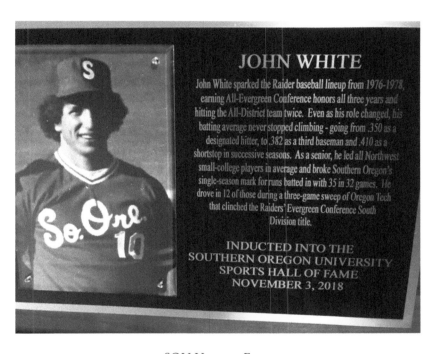

SOU Hall of Fame

Chapter 8

*T*here are lessons in all we do. We only have to look for them. What follows are more true anecdotes from my life that have taught me valuable life lessons that I often share with the players on my teams. After 64 years of being a player, a coach, or both, I have encountered a wide array of experiences following what I am the most passionate about...learning and teaching life lessons through sports.

When you read articles these days that are written to help you be a better coach or player, there are always tons of buzzwords and phrases. Respect, responsibility, commitment, work ethic, focus, staying in the moment, dedication, team bonding, and other similar terms have been used so often they seem to have lost their effectiveness. So, in addition to teaching sound fundamentals, my emphasis has been to try to bring back the joy of playing to my teams and to the players on my teams. Players in all four of the high school sports I have coached (baseball, softball, basketball, and volleyball) have reacted well to this approach. They have formed close personal and team attachments, have become more competitive, and have enjoyed coming to practice every day. We don't do it all the time, but we have several short competitive games we made up that brighten smiles, stir competitive juices, create conditioning in a non-traditional way, and keep the kids engaged. It keeps practices from being too repetitive and keeps the interest level up.

This approach goes back to my own experiences. There was a backstop near my home when I was growing up. The kids in the town of Eagle Point would congregate there nearly every day during the summer, often until dark. We would pretend to be big leaguers, which we would loudly announce before approaching the plate. We would play Home Run Derby, Over the Line, and various other games we made up.

When I wasn't at the backstop, I was at my grandparents place on "B"St, now Shasta Avenue. They lived on Little Butte Creek and had a small sandbar directly behind their house. There was always gravel on the sandbar that I would hit with an old axe handle or a broom handle into the pools farther down the stream. If the stone did not land in one of the 4 pools (single, double, triple, home run) it was an out. I would play complete 9 inning games. In later years, I continued to hit gravel into a field behind our house. When we arrived at our new home on Stevens Rd, I was in the 8th grade and there was a five yard gravel pile beside the house. When I graduated from Eagle Point High School 5 years later, it was more like a two yard pile.

Being inside was something that was rare for me as a kid, and even later on. If it wasn't baseball, it was basketball on the local outdoor courts, tennis, ping-pong, or football on the high school field. We walked to the fishing holes, picked blackberries to sell or make into pies, and rode bikes to the local pool. We never worried about predators and our parents never worried about where we were.

This approach to life continued on when I entered the United States Air Force after a year playing baseball at Pacific University in Forest Grove, Oregon. My family was not well-off. In fact, we were always just scraping to get by. My highly intelligent brother, Greg, who was still in high school and my sister, Terria (who was Down's Syndrome)were enough of a financial obligation for my parents, especially considering that my mom was still finishing up her master's degree in English at Southern Oregon College (now SOU). Pacific was just too expensive, even with a sizable scholarship.

I decided to take a chance at not getting drafted by the military. It didn't work. My birthdate was pulled at number 11, a number that was guaranteed to be drafted early. I joined the Air Force and got sent for 15 months to Chinese Language School at the Defense Language Institute in Monterey, California, followed by an additional 4 months of Chinese military training at Goodfellow AFB in San Angelo, Texas. President Nixon normalized relations with China shortly before I finished training and the Air Force suddenly had too many Chinese spies. That turned out to be very good for me.

As soon as I got to Texas, I tried out and made the base fast pitch softball team. Because Goodfellow AFB wanted to keep me in San Angelo to play ball and because I had a top secret codeword security clearance, the command staff was able to transfer me into a mobile security squadron at Goodfellow. Our job was to go to war games, test new listening devices and communication equipment, and be ready to deploy quickly in case of war. My job became teaching truck driving for 4 hours every morning. To fill up the rest of the day and avoid picking up cigarette butts at the barracks, I spent much of the day at the gym playing basketball, football, racquetball, tennis or volleyball. When I wasn't there, I was at the golf course.

And, I became a shortstop on a local town baseball team that played doubleheaders every Sunday between March and October all over Texas and Mexico. The players were all Hispanic except me and the catcher, Moose Sullinger, another Air Force guy. It was difficult learning to hit the softball correctly, but the baseball was terrific. Four of our players had played professionally, two as high as AA professionally and we were very good. We had a couple good, young, hard throwing pitchers. We had some great days and won 54 of our 62 games. I personally had a 56 game streak without an error at shortstop, had several two-homer games, and hit close to .400. I was playing so well, in fact, that Red Schoendienst, manager of the St Louis Cardinals, tried to get me released from the Air Force to sign a minor league contract. The answer from the commander was that the Air Force had spent so much money on me they wanted to get a return on their investment. At season's end, I was named MVP, but not before experiencing a frightening day in Nuevo Laredo, Mexico.

When we arrived for the games that day, it was business as usual. There was a pig roasting in a pit for the feast afterwards. Everyone was all smiles and happy to see us. The first game was uneventful and we won easily. For the second game, we started a young, wild 19 year-old righthander, who threw heat. The only problem was that he didn't always know where it was going. Sure enough, he drilled a guy in the back in the first inning. Nobody thought much of it. Then, he got another guy in the third, dropping him to his knees. The murmurs started in the stands, right about the time the third beers kicked in. Then, when he nailed his third guy in the 6th, the murmurs became an uproar. Our guys were getting a little apprehensive, especially when a large group surrounded our dugout. When we got the last out, my teammates gathered closely around me. They told me that when we left the field, I would be in the middle of the group. When I asked why, they told me it was because they were afraid I could get knifed because I was the white guy. Needless to say, when we got to the cars, I got in and drove straight home... no barbecued pork that day! Nuevo Laredo is now the hotbed of Mexican Drug Cartels and is an even more frightening place.

In the fall, I was the quarterback on the base flag football team, much like I was the year before in Monterey, California in language school. My receivers had played college football for Bowling Green, Texas Tech, and Kansas State. My running back was my good friend, Johnny Jackson. Johnny was the cousin of Lawrence McCutcheon, who was a hard-hitting back for the Los Angeles Rams. Rumor has it that the two of them were an explosive 1-2 punch in high school with little difference in talent between them. I believe it. We had a great time and won all our games.

While in San Angelo, I also played on the base basketball team. We were a high-flying fast break team that seldom scored less than 110 points a game. We went 6'9", 6'7", 6'7" across the front. All of them could rebound and all could run. The scoring guard was a 5'8" totally ambidextrous guy who had every shot...from either hand, including 20' jumpers. I was the starting point guard. I had to beat out a 6'4" all-state guard from Louisiana to get the spot. My job was to run the whole operation. We played locally at the YMCA and statewide AAU against Southwest Conference freshman teams. In those days, freshmen could not play varsity basketball on NCAA D1 teams. We played against Texas Tech, Texas A&M, Texas, and others. We finished second to Baylor in the state AAU championships. My high point game was 48, before the 3-point shot was added to the game. Mostly, I love basketball and understand it well. However, it is often the most frustrating sport to coach and play because it is much more a team game than some players want to believe. Timing is incredibly important as is everyone being in the right place at the right time. The night I scored 48 was not a situation where I was hot and forcing shots. I was simply splitting the top of a 2-3 zone and hitting short shots. The other team never adjusted. On other nights, it was somebody else scoring. It was a fun team!

I also played volleyball with 5 sky-walking Hawaiians. They all played above the net. I was the setter or the digger...well below the net. It was a blast. I've seen college and Olympic men's volleyball. We were not quite that, but weren't too far away.

Softball at this time for me was in the development stage. I was playing a lot, gradually getting better, but we were relatively young as a team. We played weekend tournaments, but were often knocked out in 3 or 4 games because the tournaments were double elimination and we used up our two losses too soon. We did well in one tournament, however. It was a 40 team tournament played in San Angelo. We won our first game on Friday, then lost game two.

Saturday morning, we got to the park early and started playing. It was July and got up to 115 degrees. It was so hot, they brought in a full water truck and dumped all the water between games. It dried up in 20 minutes. We just kept playing and winning...all day into the middle of the night, with one pitcher! When we finally got defeated at 3 am, we had played 7 games that day, my personal record.

Another memorable occurrence happened one day while I was still playing for this team. We were scheduled to play a double-header against a small Air Force base in a town near Lubbock, called Levelland. When we arrived, it was a beautiful day, 72 degrees and sunny with a light breeze. Just before game time, the wind picked up significantly, reaching gusts of 20 mph or higher...straight out to left field! As I came to the plate in the first inning, the wind was whipping. I hit a fly ball to left field. It carried and carried and went out of the park for a home run. That same exact thing happened 5 more times that day. I ended the day with 5 home runs and a

ground rule double. No one else, on either team, hit a ball that even had a chance to go out. I was pretty excited and called my mom shortly after the games were over. Thinking she would be excited, I was surprised when I got silence instead. She asked me to repeat the name of the town. When I told her it was Levelland, she informed me that my grandmother Lee Lucas had died there. I was silenced too.

As you can probably tell, my life was a joyful mix of competing in different sports. The variety was really rounding me into a very good athlete. But, as Grandma's favorite, the firstborn grandson, I was stopped in my tracks that day. A message?

One other thing happened in the San Angelo days. I met my future wife, Rachel Calderon, at the local Dairy Queen. She was still in high school when I met her, but there was a spark there. She always managed to take my order when I came in. She was a cutie and a hard worker. She and her friend worked the late shift.

They were often the ones tasked with closing the business at night. My friend and I were often the final customers of the day. I took Rachel out twice before my squadron moved to San Antonio. She managed to look me up and reconnect during my final months in San Antonio. She lived with her aunt and uncle very close to Kelly AFB, my final duty station. We spent the next 10 years together after getting married in April of 1975. She came from a very close knit, large Hispanic family. There was always activity going on. She was a very good woman, but there were very few Hispanics in the valley when she moved to Oregon with me and I think she was always homesick for Texas. Ironically, there are many Hispanics in the Rogue Valley now.

Chapter 9

A friend recently uttered the well-known phrase "It is what it is, until you decide to change it". I started to think about that and suddenly realized that change is the key word in that phrase. Change is an open door anyone can walk through on any day, both forward and backward. It depends on what you choose. Or, you can choose to never change. It applies to teams and individuals equally.

In 2005, at Rogue River High School, the baseball team was exceptional. It hadn't always been that way. When I arrived in 2002 for a coaching job, the situation was pretty bleak. The team had won a total of 8 games over the previous 4 years combined. We ended up starting 6 freshmen that year. They worked hard and for the next 2 years, improving from 9-17 in 2002 to back-to-back 16-10 years in both 2003 and 2004.

The 2005 team featured 7 senior starters. We played in the toughest 3A league in the state (there were 4 divisions at the time - 1A, 2A, 3A, and 4A). That team went 23-4 overall in a league that featured 4 of the top 6 teams in the state. Those boys won the Skyline Conference that year because they refused to be second to anybody. They made the change over time, with great leadership, multi-sport athletes, and an unequaled competitive nature. They even ran handstand races at practice...from third to home. Plus, they truly cared about each other.

The 2009 team was also a winner, eventually constructing a record of 20-7 after a 2-5 start. The previous two years had been winning years, but were nothing special. This team had only 3 seniors, but had incredible leadership, primarily from my son Kelly and his fellow senior, Craig Lee. They would just look at one of our 6 freshmen, and positive things would happen. We refused to lose and won the 8-team Sunset League championship. So, change happened. Kelly became the first Chieftain to be a first-team all-state selection in more than 20 years. He hit over.500 and led the state in Runs Batted In (RBI). Three teammates, Craig, Brendan Schoner, and Christian Reyes were second team selections. Those four drove in more than 70% of our runs and were instrumental in my being named as the state's coach-of-the-year. That year also provided one of the biggest highlight moments of my coaching career.

As a dad, there were moments that arose once in a while about whether I was favoring my son. I tried to treat him even a little tougher than I did others as a result. One day Kelly's senior year, all that toughness was paid back in full. Rogue River was tied with Cascade Christian at 12-1 going into the final game of the 2009 season. The winner of that game would win the Sunset League title. Rogue River jumped out to a 5-0 lead in the first inning. Kelly hit a hard smash down the third base line that was ruled an error that allowed 2 runs to come in. But, when Kelly came up for the second time, Cascade had fought back to take a 7-5 lead. As often happened, Brendan Schoner and Craig Lee were on base. Cascade brought in a reliever to face Kelly. The first pitch was a thigh high fastball on the inner half of the plate. Kelly jumped on it and just crushed a 3-run home run estimated at 430' to deep left field to put Rogue River up 8-7. His next trip, Cascade was up again 9-8. The same guys were on base. Kelly again crushed the ball to left. This time, it didn't go out, but hit the top of the fence and bounced nearly back to the infield, 10-9 Rogue River. We went on to score two more that inning. A meaningless run by Cascade left the final score 12-10 and Rogue River the Sunset League Champion. Kelly went on to be Player of the Year in the Sunset League and a first-team all-stater. What he and his teammates did that day also paved the way for me to be the conference Coach of the Year and the Oregonian Newspaper Coach of the Year. It's a pretty incredible feeling to be on the All-State team with your son!

Individuals can decide to change, too. I've seen many instances where this took place. Here are a few, including from me personally.

Abe Lupkin was 5'4" or so and maybe 135. He wrestled and played baseball at Phoenix High School. When I met him, he couldn't hit the ball out of the infield, had a mediocre arm, and was not a fast runner. But, he loved baseball! When I ran a year-round baseball school for the Oakland A's affiliate at Miles Field in Medford, Abe was there every day. And, I mean every day. He transformed himself into a ball player. My biggest memory of Abe was the day it was 8 degrees on our outfield thermometer. He had playground balls out and had found a spot of cleared black asphalt in the field of two inch deep snow that covered everything else. He hit off a tee for half an hour into a pocket net. Abe went on to play 4 years of college baseball, at College of the Siskiyous in Northern California and York College, Nebraska. He is a high school coach in Washington state now.

When I was a freshman at Eagle Point High School, I was the world's worst cross-country runner. In those days, we ran races at high school football halftimes. I was the youngest guy in my class and one of the smallest, with heavy legs. Football was out of the question, so I ran cross-country with my buddies. When we ran races that year, I was always last of the junior varsity guys. When we ran the halftime races, I would arrive at the finish line midway through the third quarter and would be humiliated by what I called the sympathy applause. I wanted to crawl in a hole. I went on that year to play freshman basketball and became a starter on the varsity

baseball team. When baseball was nearly finished, I decided I was going to try cross-country again, but not under the same circumstances.

I started running every day and not just short distances. By
the time the summer was over, I had logged 1000 miles. When my
teammates ran against me in practice that fall, they were astonished.
My coach, Jim Crumpton, a disciple of the University of Oregon's
Bill Bowerman and a friend of Nike's Phil Knight, was impressed
and immediately put me on the varsity team. The first race of the
year was at a football game. I finished in a four-way tie for first
with three of my teammates. This time, the applause was genuine.
This cross-country team was a dominant force for my final 3 years,
finishing in the top five of teams at the state championship race all
three years, with a best of second my junior year. The top 5 guys on
our team were very good runners. Steve Modee, who was a two-time
state half-mile champion in track, and my buddies Bob Hanscom,
Ron Peck, Terrell Bowdoin and myself often finishing well ahead of
other team's first finisher. Steve ran at the University of Oregon and
I was the number one man at Pacific University, Oregon my freshman year, maybe the only college baseball/cross-country athlete ever.

On a somewhat different note, change can happen for different reasons. One, in particular, brought tears to my eyes. A young
man, to remain nameless, was caught one year by school authorities
smoking marijuana with two girls in a shed at school. It happened
on the very day he was going to be named to the varsity baseball
team as a freshman. Three years later, having done everything by
the book in the meantime, this same young man pitched a complete
game 2-1 victory against the top pitcher in the state to win a league
championship. He is now highly respected in law enforcement.

Change happened in all these instances because at least some
individuals were unwilling to let things continue the direction they
were going. I often find myself wishing that those who have made
mistakes would wake up some morning and decide to make changes

for their own good. It can happen any time just by walking into the open door of change. It is what it is, until you decide to change it.

Chapter 10

*T*here is something about remarkable athletes that sets them apart from the rest of the competition. They love to hit a baseball or softball, everyday. They love to shoot basket after basket, everyday. They love to throw, kick, or catch a football, everyday. They love having a volleyball in their hands, everyday. They love to kick a soccer ball nonstop. They love to run, everyday. They will show up on short notice or at times others won't. They don't make excuses or blame others. They show up and work at fitness. And, eventually, they win because they possess work ethic and the willingness to do something everyday to make themselves better, including training their minds. Plus, because they are there all the time, they are completely in their element when it comes time to perform. Working at your sport constantly is what makes you improve, not constantly starting and stopping. Doing something (mentally, physically or both) positive EVERY DAY to make yourself better is the key.

That was my mental approach when I enrolled at Southern Oregon University after 4 years in the Air Force, to get better every single day. And, that's what I did. I lifted weights, ran long distance at night, hit for an hour daily, and ran a set of sprints every afternoon. And, I went to class, getting grades that allowed me to eventually graduate with honors. I loved being back in college and I loved college baseball. The results spoke for themselves. I hit really well, loved competing, enjoyed being around my teammates, trained my mind daily by always imagining positive results, and I joyfully approached each day. To make things better, we won a significant number of games.

Some of the most memorable were victories over University of Oregon and a doubleheader sweep of the University of Portland, a team that featured future major league pitchers Ken Dayley and Bill Krueger and future college coaching legend Pat Casey (Oregon State).

We destroyed Oregon Institute of Technology in a three game set my senior year to win the conference. Every time I came to the plate there were teammates on base. I drove in 12 runs that weekend. There were 340+ teams in NAIA in those days and it was nearly impossible to make All-American teams, but in my senior year I did lead Northwest small colleges in batting average (.410), extra base hits, and runs batted in (with an SOU record 38). Our team was really solid at every position, but we were not deep in pitching. We ended up losing in the first game of NAIA District Playoffs to future Willamette University and Oregon State coach David Wong. We didn't have the depth to work our way back to the championship.

My teammate Gary Glass needled me constantly with humorous digs and pushed me to be better because he was second to me in every offensive category (except walks). My competitiveness would not allow me to let him beat me.

Gary was instrumental in pushing me to bigger and better things in ASA softball too. We played together for years, primarily for Blitz of Medford, Oregon, one of the premier men's fastpitch teams in the Northwest. We both were two-time ASA All-Americans. We had great times with our softball teams. I have played in 9 National Championship tournaments in many locations: Oswego, New York; Redding, California; Boulder, Colorado; Las Vegas, Nevada (2 times); Tahoe City, California; Bakersfield, CA; Olympia, Washington and Sacramento, CA. I've also played Regional Championships in Seattle, Tacoma, Lacey and Spokane,

Washington; Boise, Idaho; Billings and Missoula, Montana; and Portland, Oregon. I've played in other large tournaments in many of the same places, but also in Reno;Sacramento; San Antonio; Montgomery, Alabama; and Houston...most of our expenses were picked up by our sponsors. None of that would have been possible without teammates like Gary Glass.

Friendships and connections through college baseball and softball have been a big part of my life. I learned to really understand hitting when I played softball with Staff Sergeant Tom Jenkins, a skinny catcher who could hit anybody. My last year in Texas in 1974 was a testament to that acquired knowledge. I was very successful playing in a 14-team league that featured three different pitchers who had been All-World at one time or another. When I arrived back in Oregon the following year, I was primed for success. I played a ton of games and seemed to never stop hitting, including 36 home runs that first year back in Oregon, 1975. From the moment I arrived in Medford in April of 1975 until I quit playing for good in 1998 at the Nike World Master's Games, softball was a huge part of my life...and still is as a coach.

My teammates on the Lithia Allen team have been lifelong friends. Lloyd Campbell not only was a pitcher on that original Lithia-Allen team in 1975, but subsequent teams that we played together. As I mentioned earlier, he won 100+ games in a row in our local Jackson County Softball Association league. The hitters bailed him out a few times, but mostly he was that guy who could find a way to win. When I coached high school softball, he was the pitching coach. Throughout everything, he was always there for young pitchers, always talkative but never seeking credit for success.

One of my favorite Lloyd stories happened on the first day of fishing season one year. My brother Greg joined us for opening day at Fish Lake. When we got there, the first thing we noticed was that most of the lake was iced over. But, there was an open area right off the dock that could hold maybe 10 boats. So, there wasn't much space between fishermen. Lloyd, Greg and I slid our boat onto a glassy smooth surface. There were maybe five boats on the lake and it was very quiet. We picked out a spot and dropped anchor. For a while, nobody on the lake was catching anything or even getting a bite. We were talking and laughing, but everyone else on the lake was totally silent. Suddenly, Lloyd let a small fart, just a little pffft. Immediately, his pole tip went down and he had a fish on. It was soon in the boat. Lloyd started in about how the way to catch fish that day was to fart. Soon, the exact same thing happened...a little fart, pffft, fish on. Then, soon after, Lloyd had a third fish the same way. I'm sitting there thinking that I had nothing to lose by trying. So, I managed to squeeze out a very tiny one. Bam! Fish on! Within 30 minutes, Lloyd and I had a total of 11 farts and 11 fish between us. We were dying laughing. It was an uproar. Nobody else on the lake was catching anything, including my brother. We traded poles with him, we traded positions in the boat, we changed his bait, but nothing worked. Finally, lunch time arrived and we hit the resort for hamburgers. Lloyd and I decided that Greg needed a chilburger with lots of onions and cheese. We chowed down and headed back to the lake. We had to find a new fishing spot because the other boats had overwhelmed our first spot. We anchored in a totally new location and started fishing. When we got going, Lloyd and I started right where we left off. We hauled in a few more, laughing the whole time...all with the same method as before. I looked over at my brother. He was turning bright red. The effort he was making to get that fart out was readily apparent. He strained and strained. Pffft! Bam! Fish On! I nearly fell out of the boat! Clearly, that was by far the single funniest day I have ever spent fishing. We took home our limits and I'm pretty sure nobody on that lake ever figured out what our secret was even though we had been the center of attention.

I had other teammates who also became excellent coaches. Another of my teammates, Larry Binney, was a legendary coach at North Medford High School, one of the best softball programs in the country. Mike Johnson was a highly successful coach at Crater High School. Mike Trotter was a highly accomplished pitching coach for Crater High School. George Decker spent many years with Roseburg High School and ASA programs.

Blitz Weinhard was the sponsor of our most successful teams. We had a large number of Alpha males that somehow managed to focus it all against our opponents. Warren Cooper was our larger than life catcher, Larry Binney was at first. I played shortstop and Mike Cornutt and George Decker were our usuals at 2nd and 3rd on tournament weekends. Outfielders were Gary Glass, BJ Rodgers, and Ron Webster. In the later years of our existence, Greg Glass became a great infielder for us, too. We won often because of our hitting prowess. We won the Northwest Regional tournament two years in a row, once behind the pitching of Jimmy Moore, who later became the best pitcher in the world. The second time was behind a state of Oregon legend, Mike Trotter, who ended up pitching until just a few years ago when he hung it up at the age of 79. Those two teams, in 1980 and 1981, were second and fifth in the national championship tournament. Personally, I received many accolades and awards over the years, but the teammates and the shared experiences are what I cherish most.

A young lady who exemplified the every day approach to a dream was Kortney Moore, a Rogue River High School graduate. Kortney approached me one day during PE class. She was in 6th grade and she boldly told me she was going to play college volleyball. When I gave her the every day advice, she ran with it. Every time I saw her, she was playing with a volleyball. She was a starter for 4 years at Rogue River High School and played two years at Umpqua Community College despite being in the middle of the mass shooting that happened there in 2015. She is still number 1 with me. Sorry, Anjelica, it's the best I can do! They both will know what that means, everyone else is on a need-to-know basis.

Chapter 11

I was fortunate to compete against two of the finest athletes in Oregon High School history. The first was Mike Keck from Klamath Union High School. He was named Sport's Illustrated Oregon High School Athlete of the Century and went on to become a force at Oregon State University in basketball and baseball. He was 6'2" and about 200 lbs. Legend has it that he was in the gym daily every summer with his dad Al Keck, KUHS head basketball coach. Or, he was playing baseball or football. The result was a 54 point basketball game against Crater before the 3-point shot, the best high school hitter I ever played against, and the quarterback of the year in the state. At Oregon State, he led the PAC-8 in hitting his sophomore year and was the second-leading scorer on the basketball team behind Freddy Boyd. Rumor has it he was also in line to be quarterback in football. His exploits are beyond compare, but the thing that always stood out was how comfortable he was. He was a great guy and I almost cried when he died in a car wreck his junior year at Oregon State.

Everyone knows the exploits of Oregon's greatest runner, Steve Prefontaine. He set a national 2-mile high school record, won numerous high school state championships, and became the University of Oregon's best ever long distance runner. My encounter with him was brief, but memorable.

My Eagle Point High School cross-country team traveled to the coast to run a dual meet against Brookings High School in the fall of 1967. As we prepared, before attacking the course on an old airstrip just south of the Winchuck River on the Oregon/California border, an extra runner showed up. It was unusual because he had no school markings on his white singlet or on his purple shorts. I asked our coach who he was and was told he was just an unattached runner. When we took off from one end of the runway, it quickly became surreal. I was near the front of the pack and it looked like the unattached runner was floating away from us, his feet not even touching the ground. Needless to say, we all lost sight of him as he rounded the corner at the end of the runway. I finished in the top 3 or 4 in the race, then looked around for this guy. I didn't see him until I realized he was already cooled down and was totally relaxed standing there in his sweats, completely in his element. I walked up to him and asked who he was. He told me he was Steve Prefontaine from Marshfield. He won the state A-1 cross-country championship that fall and went on to run an 8:41 2-mile in track season for a national record. Sadly, Pre also lost his life in a far too early automobile mishap.

Many of the athletes I have coached over the past 40 years have accomplished great things. Paige Leeper, my shortstop at Eagle Point the first two years coaching softball at the school for the second time, had one of the biggest moments ever. As a junior shortstop for Southern Oregon University, she crushed a grand slam home run in the do-or-die 2019 NAIA National Championship game to help lead the Raiders to their first ever national championship. Paige was a leader in every sense for me. She was a great student, was involved in student government, and was always the one you wanted at the plate when a big hit was needed. What was unusual about her was the fact that she was a one sport athlete, unless you count the off-season where she set up camp in the weight room. Most of the athletes I have coached were multiple sport participants. She was the exception, but she didn't cheat herself.

Bill Rowe and Ryan Gipson had spent hundreds of hours hitting my batting practice throws at the baseball school. They both had a dream of playing college baseball at the highest level. Ryan spent two years at Shasta College in Redding, California before ending up at Oregon State for his final 2 years. Bill spent his first 3 years of eligibility at University of California Santa Barbara before he also ended up at Oregon State. That's where they were playing when my son and I went to see them play against UCLA in the spring of 2006. They won that day to win the conference championship and they kept winning, ending up in the College World Series. When the dust settled, Oregon State was the National Champion and the winning run against North Carolina involved those two guys. Bill was on second base when Ryan hit a ground ball to the second baseman. Ryan busted his butt to first base while the second baseman fielded the ball cleanly. When he looked up and threw, the throw was a little up the line, but playable. North Carolina had inserted a back-up catcher who could not handle the throw and it went by him to the backstop. Bill scored easily. It didn't hurt that North Carolina's first baseman, the backup catcher, had atrocious footwork, but it was an all-time highlight of Beaver baseball.

The 1981 Eagle Point Baseball team was mostly seniors. At the time, they played in the Southern Oregon Conference with the biggest schools in the area. As a brand new hitting coach this team spoiled me. The work ethic was extraordinary. Extra, daily 6 am practices were the order of the day. They took a back seat to no one. They had all been freshmen, looking on as the school's 1978 team had gone unbeaten on the way to an AA state championship. Slick fielding and hard-hitting left-handed pitcher/first baseman Bryan Herrmann went on to play at Butte College and Washington State. Mark Winner, the right handed pitcher of our duo was tough as nails. He went on to star at Taft College in central California, and was a top winter draft pick before an injury slowed him. Mike Beagle, the speedy centerfielder, played baseball and football at Southern Oregon University and is now the Alumni Director at SOU. Wes Hamner and Mike Hammond were a deadly double play duo, Cliff Hoover and Pat Kilroy completed our outfield and everyone else fit comfortably into the roles they were asked to play. The key element to this team was that none of the players were ever satisfied. The entire group was driven by a "one more, coach" attitude. They managed to go deep in the state playoffs.

Two of the coaches of the 1981 team were Jay Greb and Greg Glass, Gary's younger brother. The head coach was Tom Britton, who had been pitching coach for the 1978 Eagle Point state championship team. I joined them as hitting coach, my first year as a high school coach. Greg had been 10-0 on the mound for the 1978 team and was named state player of the year. He was joined on the first team all-state team by Jay. Both of them had short professional careers. Greg went on to become an outstanding Fastpitch softball player, playing on many of our Blitz and Batzer Construction teams as a shortstop and third baseman. He was a great defensive player and had some outstanding tournaments as a hitter. Along with Gary Glass, Lloyd Campbell, Mike Cornutt, Jimmy Moore, and Butte Falls legend Darwin Moore, he was named to the 2020 State of Oregon USA/ASA Hall-of-Fame. Mike Trotter, Larry Binney, George Decker, and myself were already in. I became a member in 2001. A strong case can also be made for other members of our team that are not in yet; Warren Cooper, Ron Webster, and BJ Rodgers.

Cole Watson was my son's best friend beginning during their time together at Rogue River Middle School. As a 6th grader, he was definitely lacking in self-esteem. He was uncertain in baseball and basketball, but when track entered the picture he discovered that he had a gift. By the time he was a high school freshman everything had changed. He had become a superb baseball player, was a demon on the basketball court, and was untouchable as a long-distance runner.

We sat down one day that year to talk about his future. He could have become a college level or better outfielder, but his heart was in running. He made a great choice. He won 9 state championships in different running events, ran at University of Oregon and for the USA Mountain Running National Team (not for the faint of heart).

Chapter 12

Many obstacles stand in the way of athletes. Sometimes they are barriers they have erected in their own minds, sometimes they are physical, sometimes they are the perceptions of other people, and sometimes they are out of their control.

The mind is an incredible asset if used properly, or a hindrance if you don't. I have two personal experiences that might drive that thought home. The first occurred the summer after my junior year in high school. I had always been a very good hitter at every level, but that season was a real test. I was a 16 year old starting third baseman on the Central Point Cheney Studs AAA American Legion team. I hit for a fairly high average, but I had a major strikeout problem. And, every time I struck out it got in my head so badly that I really worried about it. It got so bad that it became a big-time emotional wall for me, even leading to tears at times. I set a new team record for strikeouts and could not seem to ever get the emotions under control that season.

It could have destroyed me, but I came up with a solution. Every morning that fall and winter and sometimes other times during the day, I would take the time to remind myself that I would never strike out more than 10 times in a season as long as I played. Guess what, I never did...not once in the next 30 years of playing ball. That reminder served as a catalyst to change my entire approach at the plate. I became more aggressive, didn't take pitches I could hit hard, and generally made contact all the time. Some seasons were better than others, but my senior year at SOU was the best. I struck out once in 145 at-bats, on a left-handed slider that I foul-tipped.

The second experience was one of the most humbling times of my life. I had played exceptionally well as a shortstop for Kelly Air Force Base in 1974, so well in fact that I was named the Most Valuable Player in the 14-team league. Before the league championship game between my division champion team and the champion of the other division, I was presented a trophy that must have been 5 feet tall. It was a powerful moment, especially because one of the prettiest and most awesome girls in San Antonio was there to watch. She had long dark hair, gorgeous blue eyes, loved watching sports, and had an incredible personality.

I took the field with a satisfied feeling. The game itself was tight throughout between two very good pitchers. Going into the bottom of the 7th inning, we were on defense in a 1-1 game. I was due up first in the top of the 8th inning and when we got the first two outs, I was daydreaming about my upcoming at-bat. I was still thinking about what I was going to do when a guy walked. Then it happened, a ground ball was hit right at me and sure enough, I pulled my glove up too soon and the ball rolled through and stopped right in the middle of the perfect triangle between me, the left fielder and the centerfielder. The runner on first was flying around the bases and ended up scoring...walk-off error. Our season was over. We didn't get to go to the regional championship, and I felt totally humiliated in front of a girl I really liked. After that day, I can truthfully say I was always in the moment and never had a ball go through the wickets that I didn't touch. My mind would just not let it happen.

Megan Ayres was a pitcher at Eagle Point when I got there in 2015 for my second time around. Her mother, Kim, was a top-notch pitcher at EPHS during my first coaching stint in the 1980s. Megan was also a great pitcher, but had a major difficulty beating one of our opponents, Marist High School from Eugene. We lost both games, home and away, for two straight years. In one game her junior year, Marist had knocked her out of the game with career home run days by two or three of their players. Marist had at least 6 future D-1 players, led by Lauren Burke, one of the top players in the country and two-time Oregon Gatorade Player of the Year.

When undefeated Marist arrived at Eagle Point Megan's senior year, the Eagles were second in the league behind Marist. Megan told me before the game she was going to beat them. She was sharp that day, we played well behind her, and she stayed in the moment. The result was an emotional 4-2 win.

Andrew Bartels came to the baseball school when he was in the 7th grade. The very first thing he asked me was what he needed to do to become a Major League Baseball player. Like I usually do, I told him to take care of his schoolwork, take care of his family and his personal situation at home, then do something every single day to get better. From that point forward, I saw him nearly every day. He would get up early in the morning and make sure his school work was done. Then, he had extraordinary focus at school, went to team practices for basketball or baseball. He would come to the baseball school to hit, take ground balls, and to lift at the gym. He hit over 100,000 balls in 6 years, he caught thousands and thousands of ground balls, and he got better and better. His senior year at Phoenix High School, he was the third leading basketball scorer in the state behind Luke Jackson (Creswell High and the University of Oregon) and Derek Anderson (Scapoose High, Oregon State and NFL quarterback). He was also first team all-state in baseball and had a 4.0+ grade point average. He was a terrific athlete, but he had an unusual vision problem. He had a degenerative condition that created difficulty in depth perception, which was a real problem, especially on pop-ups. He could not tell when the ball was coming down. But, like we always say, it's about the journey not the destination. His gpa got him ranked high enough to get the President's scholarship at prestigious Willamette University where he also played 4 years of baseball. He is now a successful administrator at a large healthcare company.

Brendan Schoner was a starting outfielder for me at Rogue River for 4 years, and was always a terrific outfielder. His first two years he was a sub-standard hitter and often hit in the nine hole. But, he suddenly overcame his mental block about hitting and became a force. He finally decided that he was a hitter. It was almost miraculous. We put him in the lead off spot, and he performed like gangbusters. When the season ended, he was a .426 hitter, stole bases nearly every game, played great in center field and ended up second team all-state. The next year he hit over .500 and was first team all-state.

Gillian Willis had a very similar path to Brendan's. She was starting second baseman for Eagle Point Softball her first two years, where she was an excellent defensive player, but not a great hitter. When All-State shortstop Paige Leeper graduated, Gillian moved to shortstop and flourished. She hit about .430 her junior year and when she was a senior, she was one of the top 3 or 4 hitters in the state, hitting over .600. She was also a first team all-state selection.

Christian Reyes was an outstanding baseball player, but had his heart set on playing NCAA D-1 football. He was a great football player at Rogue River, leading the state in rushing yards. He worked tirelessly in the gym lifting weights to get bigger because the college teams told him he wasn't big enough. He ran sprint workouts on his own because the big-time schools like the University of Oregon told him he wasn't quite fast enough. He got married early, right after high school, to his wife Kacey. They had and still have a strong bond. She became his biggest supporter. He worked his way through College of the Siskiyous in Weed, California, always maintaining his unequaled work ethic. After two years of community college football, it turns out he was big enough and fast enough to play D-1.

He became a 1,000 yard rusher at Charleston Southern in South Carolina. Nobody ever deserved success more.

On December 11, 2008, I was a varsity assistant coach and my son Kelly was a senior post player on the Rogue River High School basketball team. Kelly was running the wing full speed on a fast break. As he caught the ball and went up for a lay-in, he was jostled by two defenders. He landed awkwardly on the outside edge of his heel, and his entire foot rotated to an upside down position off the talus bone on the bottom of the foot. He could actually see the bottom of his foot as he lay on the floor. Spectators were horrified, but he was calm as a cucumber. When we got to the hospital, he was sedated and the orthopedist popped the foot back into place. There was no break, but there was considerable soft tissue damage.

When we met the doctor the next day, he was told it would be 14 weeks before he could be back at sports. 14 weeks would have made the return around April 1, well into baseball season. But, that doctor didn't know Kelly. Religiously, 5 times a day, 7 days a week, he did ice immersion treatments for 10-15 minutes each time. He kept the swelling down and he only missed one practice, a doctor's visit. In 7 weeks, he was back on the basketball court. He played on senior night and in a state playoff game. He started baseball on time and had a spectacular year. But, probably the most important thing was the respect he earned from everyone at the school. He was able to guide his senior year baseball team to a league championship because of that respect. Kelly went on to play college ball at Shasta College, where he hit over .362 each of his two years. His career was upended by a hand injury, but the journey was pretty fun.

I have spent a lot of time with all these athletes and quite a few others that were successful. But, I must stress that each and every one of these young people did the work to achieve their goals. And, they were the product of a number of excellent coaches, not just me.

Here's a list of some, but not all, of those other athletes who earned success, all winners in my book...
Rob Folsom
Steve DeClerck
Chuck Shine
Mike Newmann
Kylene Briggs
Miyah Smith
Samantha Thompson
Titus Weston
Mike Allen
Most of the starters on the 2000 4A state championship team Crater and the runners-up North Medford - constant participants at the baseball school.

Chapter 13

*T*he most valuable lesson I have ever learned from sports is that having a dream or a goal is a great thing and wonderful results may occur, but only if you understand that the destination may end up being a different place than you envisioned. In the long run, it truly is about the journey, not the final destination.

From a very early age, my dream was to become a Major League Baseball player. If the truth is told, I probably ended up with the skills to do that. But, because of things beyond my control, it never happened. I found out that timing is everything. The Kansas City Royals were interested in me in 1970 when I went to a tryout camp. The next day they were no longer interested when my military draft number came up #11. That draft number would ensure that I would be drafted into the military the following January.

The Cardinals couldn't get the USAF to release me from my military obligation when they were interested in signing me and when I got out of the Air Force, the Seattle Mariners told me I was too old even though I was a very good prospect.

But, I have no regrets. My life has been very interesting, and I am happy being a coach for the past 41 years. My college baseball career at Southern Oregon was awesome. And, my ASA Softball experience was incredible. Regional and National tournaments are memories that are etched in my mind. What can be bad when you are playing ball?

I like to think that I have made a difference in many lives, but I have to stress that coaches only provide direction. Each and every successful athlete has succeeded because of things they have done personally. Coaches are able to develop relationships with athletes that no one else can. You can't possibly have influence over everyone you contact, but the ones you do always have a place in your heart.

I have been married to two great women. Rachel, the first, is the mother of my oldest daughter, Jennifer. Jennifer was a very good young softball player between the age of 6 and 15 when she lived with me, but gave it up when she moved to Texas with her mother as a high school freshman. Jennifer is a strong, independent businesswoman with many close friends and is the mother of my two grandchildren, Lucas and Marcus.

My second wife, Darlene, is a beautiful, sassy redhead with a quirky sense of humor. She had touched my life quite a few times without me really realizing it. The first time was at a party when I was in college. My flag football team had won the intramural championship and we decided to celebrate at the house of one of the guys. Somehow, Darlene and I ended up talking for a while downstairs while her girlfriend was hanging out with a guy upstairs. She left quickly when her friend became angry with the upstairs guy. Since she was still a senior in high school and I was married, I put it out of my mind. That next fall, I ran into her again. I always walked out of the SOU gym down a long corridor that bordered the auxiliary gym. She would be in the auxiliary gym practicing dancing. She was an amazing dancer and I would sometimes stop and watch for a few minutes. Then, she got a job at KFC. I was a big fan of chicken and stopped often. She was always a little amusing. Then, she went away, got married and ended up in California. Strangely enough, I never put any of these encounters together in my mind until we talked about it much later. The next time I saw her, she was back in Oregon, working as a runner for a title company. I was drawn to her because she looked so sad. It turns out she was very sad. She had lost a full-term baby, was grieving and then her husband had walked out. A friend of mine set us up. We talked for hours. She was often sad, but when she smiled it was a ray of sunshine. I couldn't resist. Darlene is the mother of my two younger children, son Kelly and daughter Rylee. And, she brought her laughing, caring daughter Jessica into our household. It was a full, active house from the beginning. Even though I am no longer with either wife, I would not trade my life with them for anything.

Kelly and I shared some truly special moments in baseball and basketball. He calls me for advice nearly every day and we have a special relationship because we were the only guys in the house. Rylee is the family's mother hen. She cares about everyone she meets and has many notable causes. She was a gifted softball player, but had to give it up because of time constraints. She attacks life with passion and compassion. They are both pretty awesome kids.

Baseball was my dream and I pursued it with gusto. Life took me in a different direction, but the journey has been amazing. The people I have met have also been amazing. One of the most memorable was MLB Hall-of-Fame infielder Harmon Killebrew of the Twins. I spent an entire day with him. He came to Medford to talk to the baseball school kids and then make an appearance with dignitaries at the minor league game that night. He spent several hours during the day talking baseball to the high school kids, who listened intently to his very good advice. When we took a break, I went home to pick up my seven year old son, Kelly. When we came back, we walked over to the roped off dignitary area and sat down. Harmon extricated himself from the mayor and others to come talk to my son. He sat down and legitimately talked baseball with Kelly for a full 20 minutes while the adults waited. When they finished talking, he signed a baseball that says "To my Pal, Kelly...Harmon Killebrew HOF '84". And, he meant it. Kelly just turned 30, but that ball is still one of his most prized possessions. Through the course of my travels, I have met dozens of Major League Baseball players, many of them terrific guys, but the now-deceased Harmon Killebrew stands alone when it comes to our house.

Pursue your dreams no matter what they are, roll with the punches, and continue getting after it. When it is all over, look back with happiness. It will be the people you have known and the journey you remember most. When the dream no longer holds your full attention and you have decided it is time to step away, look back on your journey fondly, knowing you have lived and embraced life to the fullest. The Coronavirus, Covid-19, will at some point become an afterthought and things will return to a new normal. Sports will not go away. There are too many lessons to be taught through sports. They will always be a part of the fabric of American life.

There is no question that the return of high school sports will be a vital part of recovering from the pandemic that has faced us. A Friday night football game that allows communities to gather, a raucous basketball game on a cold Saturday night, a quickly moving volleyball match, or an afternoon doubleheader all provide welcome relief from our busy American life. These activities are part of who and what we are and have been sorely missed by a large segment of our society. Their return with spectators will signal a return to a semblance of normalcy. Until that happens, we will all worry and wonder how our young people are handling things psychologically.

There is no doubt that I would love to coach another 10 years and that is my current dream. I don't know where my path will take me, but I know that I have the passion to continue trying to make a difference, if my body cooperates. With the interactions I expect to have with young athletes, I believe I will always feel young. I will never have regrets about the path I chose. Even though it never brought wealth or major league fame, I could never trade away the feelings that came with helping young people achieve success. It truly has been about the journey, a journey that has yet to end. Go Eagles!

CPSIA information can be obtained
at www.ICGtesting.com
Printed in the USA
BVHW051106260421
605873BV00019B/2469